Barbara Frank-Job

Immigration as a Process

Temporality Concepts in Blogs of Latin American Immigrants to Québec

INTER-AMERICAN STUDIES
Cultures – Societies – History

ESTUDIOS INTERAMERICANOS
Culturas – Sociedades – Historia

Volume 27

Barbara Frank-Job

Immigration as a Process

Temporality Concepts in Blogs of Latin American Immigrants to Québec

WVT Wissenschaftlicher Verlag Trier
Copublished by
UNO University of New Orleans Press

Immigration as a Process:
Temporality Concepts in Blogs of Latin American Immigrants to Québec /
Barbara Frank-Job. –
(Inter-American Studies | Estudios Interamericanos; 27)
Trier: WVT Wissenschaftlicher Verlag Trier, 2021
ISBN 978-3-86821-820-6
New Orleans, LA: University of New Orleans Press, 2021
ISBN 978-1-60801-215-2

SPONSORED BY THE

Federal Ministry of Education and Research

The project, on which this book is based, has been funded by the German Federal Ministry of Education and Research (Bundesministerium für Bildung und Forschung, BMBF). The responsibility for the content of this publication lies with the author.

Cover Image: Leo Reynolds, Clocks 06; https://www.flickr.com/photos/lwr/24894705383/;
Creative Commons License (CC BY-NC-SA 2.0)

Cover Design: Brigitta Disseldorf

Library of Congress Cataloging-in-Publication Data
Names: Frank-Job, Barbara, author.
Title: Immigration as a process : temporality concepts in blogs of Latin American immigrants to Québec / Barbara Frank-Job.
Description: Trier : Wissenschaftlicher Verlag ; New Orleans, LA : Copublished by UNO University of New Orleans Press, 2021. | Series: Inter-American studies ; volume 27 = Estudios interamericanos | Includes bibliographical references.
Identifiers: LCCN 2020044530 | ISBN 9781608012152 (paperback)
Subjects: LCSH: Latin America--Emigration and immigration. | Latin Americans--Québec (Province) | Latin Americans--Blogs--Québec (Province) | Immigrants--Blogs--Québec (Province)
Classification: LCC JV7398 .F73 2021 | DDC 305.868/0714--dc23
LC record available at https://lccn.loc.gov/2020044530

Publisher: WVT Wissenschaftlicher Verlag Trier, Postfach 4005, D-54230 Trier,
Bergstraße 27, D-54295 Trier, Tel. 0049 651 41503, Fax 41504, www.wvttrier.de, wvt@wvttrier.de

Copublisher: University of New Orleans Press, 2000 Lakeshore Drive, Earl K. Long Library,
Room 221, New Orleans, LA 70148, United States, 504-280-7457, unopress.org

To Christopher

Table of Contents

1. Introduction 1

2. Immigration Policy and Temporality: "Votre parcours d'immigration" 9

3. The Appropriation of the Immigration Process: Meaning Constructions of Temporality by Immigrants 32

4. Narrations of the Immigration Process 46

4.1 Narrative Appropriation of the Temporal Structures of Immigration 48

4.2 Narrations of Stages and the Collective History of Immigration 51

4.3 Putting Narrative into Perspective, Positioning and Constructing a Collective Identity 66

4.4 Narrations on the Experience of Temporality in Immigration 76

5. Blogging about the Immigration Process as a Therapeutic Coping Strategy 82

6. Conclusion 111

7. Annex: Overview of the Blogs Used 113

8. Works Cited 114

1. Introduction[1]

This essay is based on the analysis of a corpus of mostly Hispanophone blogs on the topic of immigration to Québec, comprising more than 3000 pages, which were put online between 2004 and 2017, as well as the online communication of the official (French) Canadian institutions of immigration.

The authors of the blogs come from the numerous Hispanophone countries of origin in Latin America and are in the most diverse stages of their immigration process: from potential immigrants interested in emigrating to Québec who exchange information with more experienced immigrants and get an idea about the process, to immigrants at the most diverse stages including freshly immigrated ones, to immigrants already successfully integrated into French-Canadian society, who in retrospect describe, narrate, and comment on their long journey on the basis of selected experiences and topics.

In their descriptions and narratives, the bloggers trace the entire immigration process in their own words, from the decision to emigrate to the gradual passage through various preparatory steps to immigration itself. This in turn is presented as a long process of individual stages of integration, which only comes to a narrative conclusion with the acquisition of Canadian citizenship.

The immigration process, as presented in blog entries, is accompanied interactively by more or less regularly participating actors who comment on it. A continuous communication process lasting several years comes about in which the immigrant actors construct different concepts of temporality, in some cases reflecting and discussing them. From this perspective, immigration is defined as a sequence of stages in a comprehensive process that is both the motor and the basis of processes of change in feelings of identity and the appropriation of new identities. As a result, these constructions help immigrants who are interacting to make sense of the immigra-

1 I am deeply indebted to my colleague Stephan Gramley for his important contributions and for providing a revision of the English text.

tion process as a whole and of the challenges, personal disappointments, or injuries it poses and to cope with them.

Against the background of Michel de Certeau's reflections on the identity policy content of the actions of everyday actors in the context of given institutional structures (de Certeau 1990) and taking into account the results of current research from clinical conversation analysis (Opp, Frank-Job, and Knerich 2015; Opp and Frank-Job 2017) and psychological narrative research on the therapeutic significance of verbal interaction via biographical experiences (Lucius-Hoene and Deppermann 2004a and 2004b; Neuner, Schauer, and Elbert 2009; Schauer, Neuner, and Elbert 2011; Scheidt, Lucius-Hoene, and Stukenbrock 2015), this essay understands this process of constructing meaning as a method in which the participants appropriate and work on the institutionally given directions and structures of immigration and thus also process and cope with problematic and stressful experiences on the path of immigration. These theoretical contexts will be explained in the following.

The fact that temporality plays an important role in the blogs of immigrants is not surprising. After all, the immigration process represents a long, new period in the biography of every immigrant, which makes changes perceptible and also makes painful adaptation processes necessary. Nevertheless, we were surprised to see how multi-layered, creative, and, above all, how important for identity construction the concepts of temporality among immigrants have proved to be in the course of our corpus studies.[2]

This finding leads us to the very special heuristics within the situation of blogging immigrants on the one hand and the important role of interaction in the formation of (concepts of) identity on the other.

It is known from the sociology of knowledge that biographical upheavals, to which we can count immigration, are heuristically par-

---

2 I would like to thank Nicole Drees-Alvarez and Alba Crespo Ruiz, who have collaborated on the development and analysis of the blogger corpus in the past years.

ticularly valuable because they involve situations in which previously assumed values, standards, and perspectives are no longer sufficient to cope with the new situation. Clearly, the individual needs special impulses to question his everyday knowledge. Alfred Schütz (1971) calls situations in which such impulses are given "problematic situations".

In problematic situations, there is often markedly increased self-reflection on the part of the participants who make commentaries on their own actions (Berger and Luckmann 1966a). It is in such a problematic situation within their biography that the immigrants find themselves who reflect on their current lives in Web 2.0 and try to design their future lives. To this end, they formulate their knowledge of values, life circumstances, standards of evaluation, etc., and share it with others, so that in a complex process of negotiation they build up new aspects of identity in cooperation with each other.

> [T]he experience of change and of physical or moral displacement leads people to revisit and question their past inventory of identities in order to rebuild a sense of self. (De Fina, Schiffrin, and Bamberg 2006b, 345)

The fluid, contingent, composite, and self-reflexive character of identity (Antaki and Widdicombe 1998) thus becomes particularly tangible and analyzable for the immigrants themselves, but also for the academic observer.

The interactive forms of communication that have emerged in recent years on the basis of so-called social media such as weblogs, forums, or wikis have proven to be particularly valuable in the complex situation of immigration, as they enable their users to establish social relationships independently of space on the basis of shared interests and experiences (Frank-Job, Mehler, and Sutter 2013). This makes them particularly attractive for immigrants from all over the world as forms of communication which have both a spatially and temporally unlimited communicative range and also offer a shared space of virtual interaction, which is aimed specifically at a group of people interested in immigration.

An essential motivation for immigrants to communicate on the subject of immigration in virtual space is that it gives them the opportunity to present their own experiences and to get to know comparable experiences of others, to exchange with them about the significance of these experiences and thereby to broaden their own perspective. In addition to useful factual information on the subject of immigration, they receive extensive confirmation of their decision to immigrate or reconstructive confirmation of the path they have already taken in the course of the immigration process.

Furthermore, through the practice of blogging and the resulting linguistic interchanges, they assure each other of their status as immigration experts in their own cause. All this explains why immigrants prefer to use or try to create forms of communication with a pronounced cooperative character: The hoped-for confirmation requires a confirming counterpart who makes the verbalization of one's own orientations, concepts, and categories possible in the first place and reflects their value in and for the communication community. At the same time, the cooperative development of categories and concepts within the new identity serves to create a common orientation towards the given values and selection criteria of the immigration authorities. Another essential aspect of blogging, as we will see, is the epistemic power of writing, which is particularly important in relation to autobiographical writing, which immigration blogs represent in many ways:

> Consequently, it functions as a form of institution that Alois Hahn 1987, 12) has called "biographical generators": As [...] a special institution where the individual, who is not assigned to a functional system in a functionally differentiated society, but is placed extra-socially [...], can describe him- or herself as a unit [...]. (Enderli 2014, 38; my translation – B. F.-J.)

In contrast to the secret diary, the blog benefits from the interaction about the biographical experience and its intellectual treatment within the communication community. In a way similar to other forms of interactive "biographical generators" (such as confessions or psychotherapeutic conversations, cf. Hahn 1982; Enderli 2014, 39), interactive exchanges of autobiographic messages have an additional healing function: The counterpart, who is also in the process of immigration, supports and confirms in positive and supportive comments the verbal elaboration of the self-experienced and thus also facilitates its processing (Scheidt and Lucius-Hoene 2015). Finally, and as a result of these interactive negotiation processes about each person's own biographical experiences, a collective identity of the immigrants emerges in the sense of a Community of Practice (Wenger 1998; Frank-Job and Kluge 2015; Kluge 2015). This is due to the fact that the people interacting in the blog are themselves usually immigrants who have had similar experiences that is their own experiences are experienced as "shared" experiences. Such Communities of Practice come about by writing about the experience and living of immigration and the reflections that arise as a result.

From Michel de Certeau's perspective, the identity constructions of the blogging immigrants can be perspectivized as a reflex to the official immigration and integration policies of the target society of Québec. These institutionalized rules and structures subject future immigrants to a practice of attributing predetermined values. Canada's self-definition as a country of immigration with precisely defined feature rankings for immigrants and a predefined procedure of steps ("parcours") that each immigrant must go through plays an outstanding role here.

Chapter 2 presents the concepts and categories of evaluation of the official immigration policy of Canada and Québec from Michel de Certeau's cultural-philosophical point of view as strategies of power that govern the immigrants' framework of action and uses examples of concepts of temporality to show how these strategies function as orientation for blogging immigrants. The immigrants have developed processes of constituting meaning in their blogs by bringing in their own experiences in the *parcours* phase in each of its steps. They then pass them on using various descriptive and narrative procedures which they negotiate with other immigrants. In this way they discuss and possibly confirm their meaning. This can be understood as "tactics" (*tactiques*) or "uses" (*usages*) of everyday actors who encounter the given structures of immigration as "consumers" (*consommateurs*), in this way appropriating their own biographical contexts, reinterpreting them, and thus subversively redesigning them (de Certeau 1990, 52ff).

In the same way that the Maghrebian Berber in de Certeau's example (de Certeau 1990, 51f) uses his standardized prefabricated state-subsidized housing in the Paris suburb in his very own, traditional way in order to create the broadest possible scope for a life according to the customs of his homeland, and thereby, despite the unchangeable spatial conditions, arrives at unexpected and unintended solutions, the individual blogging immigrants find new, unforeseen, and for them advantageous ways of dealing with the guidelines of the immigration authority. And although they cannot change anything in the given process and rules, they adopt individual steps of the *parcours d'immigration* by describing them as their own experience, giving them their own meaning, and incorporating them as one element among many in a complex immigrant identity. In Chapter 3, we will follow this using the example of time concepts in two cases taken from our corpus.

Similar to space and spatial perceptions, constructions of space, of "in-betweenness", etc., as they have in the meantime been intensively investigated for transnationalization processes (cf. the research overview in Baynham and De Fina 2017), concepts of time and temporality are socially and culturally constructed. They are thus determined and negotiated differently by different social actors, they are changeable, heterogeneous, and highly context-dependent. We can only grasp them by means of verbalization in communicative acts, in our case in the published material of the Canadian immigration authorities and in the posts and comments in immigrants' weblogs. From the microsocial perspective of conversation analysis, the linguistic and multimedia constitutions of meaning on the part of the immigrants can be interpreted as local narrative positioning processes (Lucius-Hoene and Deppermann 2004a) and coping practices (Neuner, Schauer, and Elbert 2009; Schauer, Neuner, and Elbert 2011; Scheidt, Lucius-Hoene, and Stukenbrock 2015), which, precisely through their interactive dynamics and emergent nature, exhibit the combination of individual experience with social sharing and confirmation necessary for the construction of identity (Berger and Luckmann 1966; Hall 1996).

Temporality is therefore understood here as a "membership category" (Antaki and Widdicombe 1998, 3; Schegloff 2007), a concept derived and interpreted by the actors themselves from their direct experiences and set as relevant in communication with other migrants. Like all membership categories, the bloggers' concepts of temporality should not be regarded as given entities, but as local accomplishments (Garfinkel 2002; Schegloff 2007; Housley and Fitzgerald 2009), that is, they are negotiated "on the spot." They are not consistent in themselves, but oriented along the lines of the local communicative needs of the group members. Their analysis is based on an examination of the categorization procedures that migrants carry out in their communicative actions.

Temporality in texts and interactions has been particularly associated with the epic mode of speaking – narrating or "narrativity." According to Paul Ricoeur (1980, 169):

> I take temporality to be that structure of existence that reaches language in narrativity and narrativity to be the language structure that has temporality as its ultimate referent.

The weblogs of Latin American immigrants to Québec that we are investigating also make regular use of the possibilities of narrating to reconstruct experiences, creating a narrative time and thus depicting certain aspects of the temporal dimension of the emigration process. As we will see in Chapter 4, narration is an essential, though not the only "tactic" in the appropriation of "concepts of temporality" by blogging immigrants.

In the light of findings from clinical and psychological research on conversation, chapter 5 concludes by elaborating on the therapeutic function of the creative processes of meaning constitution in portraying, describing, and narrating experiences in the immigrant's blogs. Here, above all, the structuring and stabilizing power of the verbal constitution of meaning becomes clear, which makes it possible to jointly process and master experiences of powerlessness and being at the mercy of unchangeable institutional directions and rules of immigration. Just as the interactive narrative reconstruction of traumatizing biographical experiences helps patients to process them and thereby reduce tensions and fears, the linguistic reconstruction of stressful experiences during the immigration process and the mutual exchange of affirmative and compassionate comments in the communication community of the blogosphere facilitates the successful processing of these experiences.

In the course of our analysis, temporality proved to be an virtually ideal thematic pivot point for perspectivizing the appropriation of identity in the immigration process by the actors involved within the dominant given political rules and directions of immigration policy: The linguistic processing, adoption, and re-interpretation of concepts of temporality discussed here, as well as their communicative negotiation in the blogger community of immigrants, the reconstructive production of temporality in immigration narratives, as well as the reflective confrontation with the official discourse of temporality policies of the Canadian immigration authorities are therefore only a few examples among numerous other possible aspects that blogging immigrants reveal when dealing with "time."

2. Immigration Policy and Temporality: "Votre parcours d'immigration"

In a first approach to the phenomenon of temporality within the process of immigration, as presented in the blogs of immigrants from Latin America to Québec, it becomes apparent that they are without exception oriented towards the guiding discourse of the official immigration and integration policies of Québec, the target society.

Canada's self-definition as a country of immigration with precisely defined feature rankings for immigrants and a regulated procedure plays a prominent role here. A special ministry is responsible for this at the national level, the Ministère de l'Immigration, des Réfugiés et de la Citoyenneté (Federal Government Department Responsible for Immigration, Refugee and Citizenship Issues). It shares the tasks at regional level in Québec with the Ministère de l'Immigration, de la Diversité et de l'Inclusion (Ministry of Immigration, Diversity and Inclusion), which also takes over the communication of the official immigration policy via communication offers published on the Internet (http://www.immigration-quebec.gouv.qc.ca/fr/accueil.html): This information ranges from the classification of immigrants into categories to precise descriptions of the steps to be completed in the application process, from immigration and integration to practical advice and interactive counselling. In this way, an institutional discourse on immigration is constituted for the immigrants seeking information or those interested in immigration, which provides each immigrant with fixed rules, procedures, concepts, and categories of the immigration process and to which he or she must conform.

Among the essential elements of this official set of immigration rules are rules of attribution, over which the immigrants themselves have no influence whatsoever. In a first step of the attribution, all those willing to immigrate are assigned to one of six categories, for each of which elaborated immigration plans are specified:

- Permanent workers
- Businesspeople
- Temporary workers
- Foreign students
- Family reunification
- Humanitarian immigration

(www.immigration-quebec.gouv.qc.ca/fr/immigrer-installer/index.html)

Since the bloggers in our corpus are without exception immigrants of the first category "*Travailleurs permanents*" (permanent workers), the process applicable to the other categories does not play a role in the following. It should be stressed, however, that the classification of immigrants into one of these categories already has the character of a social evaluation on a scale of priorities on which there are more and less desirable immigration candidates, so that the various immigrant groups correlate to specific entry or immigration conditions and the associated obstacles to permanent residence in Québec. For *travailleurs permanents*, immigration to Canada is based on a point system in which points are awarded according to certain characteristics (such as age, education, and professional skills), the number of which ultimately determines the possibility or timing of immigration. The maximum number of points to be achieved is currently (as of April 2018) 1,200 points (http://www.immigration-quebec.gouv.qc.ca/fr/immigrer-installer).

Since the beginning of 2015, applicants for permanent residence permits have been obliged to register on the website of the Ministry of Immigration and create their own profile. All personal data relevant for the distribution of points, e.g. family circumstances and connections to Canada, but also French and English language skills, level of education, work experience in the country as well as outside must be disclosed in detail.[3]

The priorities of the official immigration regulations thus determines, on the one hand, a categorization of essential and preferred characteristics over less relevant or less preferred ones. Each individual immigrant has to be classified with regard to these characteristics, which determine his identity as a immigrant and, consequently, are clearly defined first and foremost by Canada's official immigration policy and must be accepted unconditionally.

How far this kind of categorization of immigrant identity goes for the individual is revealed by the terminology. For example, the actual personal assets to be disclosed in the online profile are referred to as the "personal net value" ("valeur nette personnelle") of each immigrant. The yardstick for "personal esteem" is thus determined by the requirements of the country of immigration and, as we will see, by the financial resources of the candidate.

Following Michel de Certeau, we will understand the complex structures that have to be fulfilled by the categorization of immigrants and the definition of priorities (as well as the definition of the procedures within the immigration process, which will be discussed in more detail below) as power strategies of institutionalized immigration policy. By means of these strategies, immigration policy defines its own area of validity and thus retains its own legality and autonomy within this area, for example, in relation to other social institutions, but also, of course, in relation to the danger of unregulated immigration:

> J'appelle « stratégie » le calcul (ou la manipulation) des rapports de forces qui devient possible à partir du moment où un sujet de vouloir et de pouvoir (une entreprise, une armée, une cité, une institution scientifique) est isolable. Elle postule un lieu susceptible d'être circonscrit comme un propre et d'être la base d'où gérer les relations avec une extériorité de cibles ou de menaces (les clients ou les

3 On August 2, 2018, new immigration regulations came into force in Canada. These could not be taken into account in this essay.

> concurrents, les ennemis, la campagne autour de la ville, les objectifs et objets de la recherche). Comme dans le management, toute rationalisation « stratégique » s'attache d'abord à distinguer un « environnement » un « propre », c'est-à-dire le lieu du pouvoir et du vouloir propres. Geste cartésien, si l'on veut : circonscrire un propre dans un monde ensorcelé par les pouvoirs invisibles de l'Autre. Geste de la modernité scientifique, politique ou militaire. (de Certeau 1990, 59)

> I call a *strategy* the calculation (or manipulation) of power relationships that becomes possible as soon as a subject with will and power (a business, an army, a city, a scientific institution) can be isolated. It postulates a *place* that can be delimited as its *own* and serve as the base from which relations with an *exteriority* composed of targets or threats (customers or competitors, enemies, the country surrounding the city, objectives and objects of research, etc.) can be managed. As in management, every "strategic" rationalization seeks first of all to distinguish its "own place, that is, the place of its own power and will, from an "environment." A Cartesian attitude, if you wish: it is an effort to delimit one's own place in a world bewitched by the invisible powers of the Other. It is also the typical attitude of modern science, politics, and military strategy. (de Certeau 1988, 36)

As de Certeau puts it for various historical examples, the strategic institutionalization of immigration also offers numerous advantages for the country of immigration (Canada/Québec): For example, it serves to establish independence from the contingency of the circumstances of immigration and, as we have seen above, makes it possible to identify (groups of) immigrants as objects,

> qu'on peut observer et mesurer, contrôler donc et « inclure » dans sa vision. (de Certeau 1990, 60)

> that can be observed and measured; and thus control and "include" them within its scope of vision. (de Certeau 1988, 36)

In their effects, the strategies clearly show that they are based on social power and that at the same time they represent an essential part of the institution's exercise of power (de Certeau 1990, 60), for it is primarily through them that it becomes apparent that the institution using them is a powerful one. Thus, official immigration policy clearly shows immigrants that, when they follow the path of immigration, they are entering the sphere of power of official immigration policy and must submit to its rules and structures. This subjugation is accompanied by a necessary acceptance of predetermined attributions of identity to which each individual immigrant must relate.

Michel de Certeau contrasts the concept of *stratégie*, which, as we have seen, he assigns to institutional directions and power structures, with the concept of *tactique*. This is assigned to the individual as an everyday actor, and it describes his possibilities of action within the institutional framework. The various tactics of everyday actors, here the individual immigrants who are blogging, will be dealt with in detail in the following chapters. First, however, we will focus on how the strategies of institutionally regulated immigration to Québec affect the temporality of immigration.

The structure of Canada's immigration policy not only includes the definition of different categories of (more or less prioritized) types of immigrants and the definition of desirable or undesirable characteristics for each of these types, but it also provides a specific path of immigration with a fixed time frame for each of the different groups of immigrants. For this purpose, the Immigration Service chooses the image of immigration as a *parcours* ("route"), i.e. as a predefined course, which has several well-defined steps:

> Immigrate and settle in Québec
>
> What are the first steps that I need to take? What do I need to know?
>
> To answer these questions and many others, this section of the Website recommends a typical route. You will find an overview of the procedures to follow at:
>
> (http://www.immigration-quebec.gouv.qc.ca/en/immigrate-settle/index.html)

The suggested route includes the "demarche", the direction of the route which must be taken; in the English version *démarche* shows up as the word *procedure*, which emphasizes its predetermined, routine-like nature. It is also noticeable here that an agent, an acting person who follows the *parcours*, is grammatically hidden by the impersonal formulation. From the perspective of official immigration policy, immigration thus represents a fixed course with partial objectives to be completed, whereby those who have to master the course are not addressed as individuals, but again as members of one of the set categories of immigrants.

Each category of immigrant is given a special *parcours*. For the *Skilled worker* (*travailleur permanent*), the Immigration Authority initially provides for the following eight stages:

1. Finding out about Québec
2. Know the conditions of the Regular Skilled Worker Program
3. What to do before completing your official immigration application
4. Submit an official immigration application under Mon projet Québec
5. Submit an application for permanent residence to the Government of Canada
6. Prepare before your departure for Québec
7. Proceed to Québec's reception service at the Montréal airport
8. Take steps to successfully integrate into Québec

(http://www.immigration-quebec.gouv.qc.ca/en/immigrate-settle/permanent-workers/index.html)

Each stage opens up further partial steps to be completed with fixed conditions, such as applying for a permanent residence permit (step 5 "Submit an application for permanent residence to the Government of Canada"). This step can only be taken once the immigrant has received a Québec Selection Certificate (CSQ), i.e. the acceptance of an immigration application by the Québec Immigration Service. All other steps will be taken by the Canadian Immigration Service, i.e. at the national level. The next obligatory steps are an appointment with the official doctor and the submission of the subsequently issued official medical certificate, as well as a positive confirmation of this certificate by the Canadian Immigration Authority, and a successfully completed security check (not further described in the details of its implementation) by the same agency. It is only mentioned here in passing that the immigrant has to pay the costs of the official medical and the security checks.

As we will see below (chap. 3-4), for the immigrants this results in further obligatory partial stages on the path of immigration. Only when the Selection Certificate and security checks have been successfully completed will the immigration candidate be issued with a visa for permanent residence. Finally, reference is also made to fixed deadlines for the submission of documents and the processing times needed by the administration.

The institutionally given guiding metaphor of the *parcours*, which initially appears as a combination of individual stages, presented as fixed points in space with the connections between them described as a path to be taken, in effect implies the idea of temporality, a progression in time, since it does indeed take time to progress from one stage to the next. In the official discourse on immigration, however, the perspective is not so much movement along a path as stationary milestones or conditions that must be met in order to reach a milestone (i.e. documents available, referrals booked, a medical certificate positively evaluated, i.e. again concrete facts at concrete locations). Since behind each stage a link leads to more detailed scenarios and further partial stages, the initially so catchy image of progressing over a few stages to a single clear goal is gradually distorted and peeled off to reveal a complex, hierarchical structure.

As a result, the concept of the *parcours* presented in the official discourse fits more the concept of the map used by de Certeau. It is an example of the "spatialized principle" of the power discourse, which represents the "panoptic" structural principle of spaces, behind which the distances between the points fade away.

Consequently, de Certeau's definition of institutional strategies as actions that create and establish discursive power structures and locates them institutionally, also applies to the time structures of the official path to immigration. By assigning to each individual stage and its sub-stages their fixed place in the immigration process, the *parcours d'immigration* determines institutionally the individual movements of each person within his or her *parcours*:

> Les stratégies sont donc des actions qui, grâce au postulat d'un lieu de pouvoir (la propriété d'un propre), élaborent des lieux théoriques (systèmes et discours totalisants) capables d'articuler un ensemble de lieux physiques où les forces sont réparties. […]. Elles privilégient donc les rapports des lieux. Du moins s'efforcent-elles d'y ramener les relations temporelles par l'attribution analytique d'une place propre à chaque élément particulier et par l'organisation combinatoire des mouvements spécifiques à des unités ou à des ensembles d'unités. (de Certeau 1990, 62-63)

> In sum, strategies are actions which, thanks to the establishment of a place of power (the property of a proper), elaborate theoretical places (systems and totalizing discourses) capable of articulating an ensemble of physical places in which forces are distributed. […] They thus privilege spatial relationships. At the very least they attempt to reduce temporal relations to spatial ones through the analytical attribution of a proper place to each particular element and through the combinatory organization of the movements specific to units or groups of units. (de Certeau 1988, 38)

The strategic advantages for immigration authorities of this approach of delimiting and defining stages, procedures, and conditions for compliance are obvious. They make it possible to manage immigratory flows, quantify them, and allocate quotas, and, in particular, to control the temporal structures (by means of deadlines introduced for the submission of certain documents or by means of administrative acts which regulate the number of cases that can be processed), to decide how flows can be managed in such a way that the desired number of immigrants at a given time can successfully complete the immigration process.

For our reflections on temporality structures and their significance for blogging immigrants, these predefined steps are of enormous importance because the *parcours* with its individual stages represents the framework for their personal immigration process.

This is evident, for example, in the way blogs refer to the given deadlines for the various stages and the processes established for them. Blog 6 (April 14, 2006), under the title "Proceso de emigración al Canadá," summarizes the main stages of the official route for immigration to Québec, here in English translation:

> Québec establishes the rules and requirements enshrined in immigration laws and in accordance with them selects its immigrants. An immigrant who has been selected by Québec demonstrates this by means of a document issued by the Québec government called the Québec Selection Certificate (CSQ). With this document, [...], the interested party can submit an application for permanent residence to the federal government of Canada.
>
> This turns out to be one of the tricks I like most to teach emigrants: Confident that they will obtain the CSQ, which is issued by Québec, after they have passed the interview, they must proceed immediately to apply for permanent residence to the federal government. Both events take place in the Canadian embassy building [...]. [My translation – B. F.-J.[4]]

The guidelines are very clearly presented here as irrevocable rules that provide for a clear procedure. At the same time, the procedure for Québec is praised as a particularly fast way of initiating immigration to Canada and recommended to future immigrants.

---

4 Unless otherwise stated, all translations of citation from Spanish Blogs have been made by me, Barbara Frank-Job.

It becomes apparent at first glance that the time structures which become visible in the immigration blogs are closely oriented along the lines of the corresponding specifications of the authorities. Even if in most Latin American blogs – in contrast to Francophone blogs, which, as a rule, literally adopt the image of the *parcours d'immigration* – this image is not adopted, the idea of a process is taken over. Above all, it is the predetermined stages that structure most blogs explicitly or implicitly. This can be seen particularly clearly in the tactic of the blogging of the immigrants, which consists of listing in tabular form the individual stages in retrospect with the concrete dates of their completion after successfully finishing the process.

This is found in Blog 10, for example, at the moment when the embassy announces that it has sent the visas. The author takes this final official moment of waiting as an opportunity to recapitulate all the stages in tabular form and in the last column even lists the total number of days that the process took:

> Para los ansiosos como yo que les gusta saber los tiempo de los demás…

Resúmen de Tiempos	Fecha	Días	Acum Días.
Presentac. DPI[5]	25/09/2003		
Recepcion DCS[6]	09/12/2003	75	75
Presentación DCS en Qbc	06/02/2004	59	134
Recepción Acuse recibo	25/02/2004	19	153
Notificación Entrevista	21/04/2004	56	209
Entrevista	05/05/2004	14	223

5 DPI= Demande préliminaire d'immigration.

6 DCS = Demande de certificat de sélection.

Presentación Embajada	12/08/2004	99	322
Comienzo Proces.Solic.en Emb.	01/09/2004	20	342
Status de Expediente en Internet	07/09/2004	6	348
Sobre con Forms Ex.Médicos	24/11/2004	78	426
Laboratorio y Placas	27/11/2004	3	429
Examenes Dr. [nombre]	01/12/2004	4	433
Pago Derecho de Admisión	06/12/2004	5	438
Llegada Med Checks a T&T	06/12/2004	0	438
Cambio de "In Process" a "Dec. Made"	31/01/2005	56	494
Llamado por Visas	01/02/2005	1	495

(Blog 10, January 2, 2005)

For anxious people like me who would like to know how long other people's process took

Summary of Times	Date	Days	Total of Days
Submission of DPI	09/15/2003		
Receipt of DCS	12/09/2003	75	75
Submission of DCS at Québec	02/06/2004	59	134
Receipt of acknowledgment of submission	02/15/2004	19	153
Notification of interview	04/12/2004	56	209
Interview	05/05/2004	14	223
Personal appearance at embassy	08/12/2004	99	322

Start of the request process at the Embassy	09/01/2004	20	342
Status is applicant dossier in internet	09/07/2004	6	348
Envelope with form for medical examination	11/24/2004	78	426
Laboratory and radiographs	11/27/2004	3	429
Examination by Dr. [name of doctor]	12/01/2004	4	433
Payment of admission fee	12/06/2004	5	438
Arrival of medical checks at T&T	12/06/2004	0	438
Change from "In Process" to "Completed in Dec."	01/31/2005	56	494
Telephone notification of visa	02/01/2005	1	495

In Blog 8, the table is created at the moment the visa arrives, as the last entry before departure to Québec. The list of individual stages with data is already categorized here as a routine blog entry ("resumen obligado"):

> Así quedaron las fechas
>
> Bueno, este era un resumen obligado ...
>
> - Junio 18 2004 Envío de solicitud de entrevista junto con el primer pago
> - Junio 30 2004 Carta indicando la recepción de la solicitud
> - Octubre 15 2004 Carta indicando que estamos en lista de espera para la entrevista, la carta indicaba que la entrevista era presumiblemente en mayo
> - Diciembre 10 2004 Carta convocando a la entrevista para el 9 de marzo

- Marzo 09 2005 Entrevista de selección
- Abril 19 2005 Entrega de solicitud de visa con un segundo pago
- Agosto 11 2005 Recibo de orden de examenes médicos
- Septiembre 03 2005 Realización de exámenes médicos
- Septiembre 28 2005 Carta indicando que se debe entregar el pasaporte para imprimirle la visa
- Octubre 12 2005 Pago de la visa y entrega de pasaporte
- Febrero 14 2006 Recepción de los pasaportes con la visa y confirmación de residencia permanente
- Fecha proyectada de viaje 17 de junio 2006

(Blog 8, March 15, 2006)

This is how the dates were.

Well, this was a must-have summary...

- June 18, 2004: Submission of interview request along with first payment
- June 30, 2004: Letter indicating receipt of application
- October 15, 2004: Letter indicating that we are on a waiting list for the interview; the letter indicated that the interview was presumably in May
- December 10, 2004: Letter with an invitation to an interview on March 9
- March 9, 2005: Selection interview
- April 19, 2005: Submission of visa application with a second payment
- August 11, 2005: Receipt of invitation to the medical examination
- September 3, 2005: Conduct of the medical examination
- September 28, 2005: Letter stating that the passport must be submitted for entry of the visa.

- October 12, 2005: Visa payment and passport return
- February 14, 2006: Receipt of passport with visa and confirmation of permanent residence
- Projected date of travel: June 17, 2006

Under the title "Timing: A bitter Sweet Symphony," the author of Blog 13 posts a tabular overview of the start of her immigration path up to then in which the exact dates of the partial goals reached are entered according to the officially specified stages. She and her family were at the time waiting for the medical examination instructions. She starts by explaining the purpose of the list and invites her readers to follow her example in order to facilitate the predictability of the expected waiting times:

> Aqui resumimos nuestros tiempos en el proceso. Me encantaria que en los comentarios pongan sus tiempos, si estan en proceso, para tener todos una referencia, es muy útil para los que estamos esperando la visa y para los que hasta ahora comienzan hagan sus calculos:
>
> Envio primer dossier México: 7 Febrero 2007
>
> Confirmación de apertura: 13 marzo 2007
>
> Notificacion de entrevista: 26 julio 2007
>
> Entrevista: 18 septiembre 2007
>
> Envio segundo dossier Bogotá: 12 octubre 2007
>
> Confirmación de apertura: 3 Diciembre 2007
>
> Recibo ordenes Medicas: 25 Febrero 2009
>
> Presentación pruebas médicas: 02 Marzo 2009
>
> Entrega de pasaportes a la embajada: 02 Marzo 2009
>
> Envío resultados a Trinidad y Tobago: 03 Marzo 2009
>
> LLegada de las visas: 15 abril 2009
>
> La duración de nuestro proceso tomó exactamente 16 meses desde la apertura del dossier hasta la llegada de las visas.

> Y como dicen: Bon Courage! (para ustedes y nosotros)
>
> (Blog 13, February 2009)
>
> Here we summarize our times in the process. I would love you to put your times in the comments, if they are in process, to get all the information, which is very useful for those of us who are waiting for a visa and for those who now want to begin to make their calculations:
>
> Sending first dossier from Mexico: February 7, 2007
>
> Opening confirmation process: March 13, 2007
>
> Notification of interview: July 26, 2007
>
> Interview: September 18, 2007
>
> Second dossier sent to Bogotá: October 12, 2007
>
> Confirmation of opening of process: December 3, 2007
>
> Receipt of invitation to the medical examination: February 25, 2009
>
> Presentation of medical certificates: March 2, 2009
>
> Delivery of passports to the embassy: March 2, 2009
>
> Results sent to Trinidad and Tobago: March 3, 2009
>
> Arrival of visas: April 15, 2009
>
> The duration of our process took exactly 16 months from the opening of the dossier to the arrival of the visas.
>
> And as they say: Good luck! (for you and us)

In comparison with most other immigrants from Latin America, this time span proved to be extremely fast. This may be the reason why, in the twelve comments that the blogger received in return, only a few complied with his request to provide their own times according to the same system.

The first commentator lists fewer stages; he was, at the time, between the 4th and 5th official stages and was therefore waiting for the invitation to the medical examination:

Hola B.

Te dejo mis tiempos:

Envío a Mexico Junio 2007

Entrevista Diciembre 5 2007

Radicación Embajada Diciembre 6 2007

Confirmación Febrero 25 2008

ánimo.. no podemos hacer más ;)

(Blog 13, February 2009, comment 1)

Hi B.

I'm giving you my times:

Mailing to Mexico - June 2007

Interview - December 5, 2007

Filing (of application) at the embassy - December 6, 2007

Confirmation - February 25, 2008

Good luck! ... we can't do more ;)

With the last addition, the powerlessness that the individual actor faces within the course of immigration becomes clear. The process was obviously stagnating for almost six months.

Finally, a third commentator, who had also not yet completed his immigration process but had already completed the medical examinations stated that the intervals between the stages are similar to those given in the blog. He also follows the sequence of the official stages and encourages the first commentator that he too will certainly receive an invitation to the medical examination very soon:

Hola B.

Esto es bastante ínteresante.....mis tiempos son muy similares a los tuyos

Envio primer dossier México: 28 Enero 2007

Apertura de dossier: 13 marzo 2007

Confirmación de apertura: 13 abril 2007

Notificacion de entrevista: 27 julio 2007

Entrevista: 18 septiembre 2007

Envio segundo dossier Bogotá: 20 noviembre 2007

Confirmación de apertura: 23 enero 2008

Envío de ordenes médicas: 20 Febrero 2009

Un abrazo y valor, tus ordenes ya deben estar por llegar.

(Blog 13, February 2009, comment 3)

Hi B.

This is quite interesting... my times are very similar to yours.

First dossier sent to Mexico: January 28, 2007

Opening of dossier: March 13, 2007

Confirmation of opening of the process: April 13, 2007

Notification of interview: July 27, 2007

Interview: September 18, 2007

Second dossier sent to Bogotá: November 20, 2007

Confirmation of opening of process: January 23, 2008

Invitation to the medical examination: February 20, 2009

A hug and stick with it! Your invitation should already be here by now.

These lists with their concrete data thus represent a collectively shared practice of blogging immigrants. In de Certeau's terminology it is a "tactic" intended to increase the predictability of the immigration process and thus reduce the contingency of the process, which is felt to be particularly burdensome due to the endless waiting times. At the same time, however, the implementation of this tactic makes it all the clearer how much the bloggers' activities move within the structures and rules laid down by the authorities. Their freedom is limited by the stages, and each stage they reach only seems to be a brief moment of success, a move forward on the path, perhaps with the possibility of taking an initiative on their own. However, the possibility of acting on their own, of moving the process forward or of speeding it up seems rather random, as a special opportunity that arises, as a tactic that "takes advantage" in the short term of accidental incidences in the individual process, only to fall back into the strictly defined framework immediately afterwards:

> Au contraire, du fait de son non-lieu, la tactique dépend du temps, vigilante à y « saisir au vol »des possibilités de profit. Ce qu'elle gagne, elle ne le garde pas. Il lui faut constamment jouer avec les évènements pour en faire des « occasions ». Sans cesse le faible doit tirer parti de forces qui lui sont étrangères. (de Certeau 1990, XLVI)

> On the contrary, because it does not have a place, a tactic depends on time – it is always on the watch for opportunities that must be seized "on the wing." Whatever it wins, it does not keep. It must constantly manipulate events in order to turn them into "opportunities." The weak must continually turn out [to] their own ends forces alien to them. (de Certeau 1988, XIX)

Perhaps most impressive is the extreme limitation of freedom in the individual processes on the part of the official discourse on immigration in relation to the concept of identity. Against the background of the officially propagated ideal of complete integration into the target society as a defined end point of the immigration process, this is of particular importance.

In the official discourses on immigration in Québec, identity is postulated as a static concept, as clearly defined and precisely determinable in its characteristics, as unchangeable and thus also easy to acquire. One section in the information brochure Guide pratique de l'immigration of the city of Québec, for example, presents typical characteristics and behaviors of the Québecois: "Apprendre les valeurs et l'identité québécoises" ("Learn Québec values and identity") (www.akova.ca/wp-content/themes/.../guide_ immigration.pdf).

Right away on the welcome page of the government agency there is a link to "apprendre Le Québec" ("learn about Québec"), behind which a complete accommodation program is hidden:

> The guide *Learning About Québec* can help you accomplish your project. It has two sections. The first, What you need to know, offers practical information on everything you need to know before your departure.
>
> The second section, *What you need to do*, is a personalized action plan that explains the steps you will need to take, both in your country of origin as well as upon your arrival in Québec.
>
> (http://www.immigration-quebec.gouv.qc.ca/en/informations/apprendre-quebec/index.html)

Here, too, the concept of the *parcours* with its fixed stages emerges, but they are regarded here as administrative tasks. One of these tasks is to "learn" the identity values of Québec.

The official website of the Québec Immigration Service explicitly presents the norms and values to be learned, which are "shared by all Québecois:"

> Speaking French is a necessity
>
> A free and democratic society
>
> A society enriched by its diversity
>
> A society based on the rule of law
>
> Political and religious powers are separate
>
> Men and women have the same rights
>
> The exercise of human rights and freedoms must respect the rights and freedoms of others and the general well-being
>
> (http://www.immigration-quebec.gouv.qc.ca/en/avantages/valeurs-communes/index.html)

Finally, a flyer entitled "Connaître, respecter, partager: les valeurs communes de la société Québécoise" ("Know, Respect, Share: the common values of Québec society") explaining these values is available for downloading in seven different languages.

As we will see in the following chapters, such an institutional fixation on identity is diametrically opposed to the experiences of immigrant as independent actors. In their negotiations, the processual nature of immigration, the overcoming of hurdles, reaching new stages, shared negative and positive emotions in connection with individual steps, questions and answers, objections and their refutation with regard to steps to be taken or attitudes to be adopted play an important role. Here a concept of immigrant identity as an emergent and dynamic variable becomes visible, based on experiences and feelings, mutual worries and fears, common to all and linguistically reconstructed together with others, yet often proving to be unstable and contradictory.

This confirms the contrast between the actions of institutions and actions of everyday actors, between strategies of power and tactics of use, which de Certeau emphasized so clearly.

Before we turn to the tactics of immigrants in the following chapters, as they make use of the structures of the immigration discourse given to them, it should be pointed out here that the relationship between official discourse on immigration and the provisions of the everyday actors proves to be more complex on closer examination than the clear juxtaposition of institution and everyday actor in de Certeau, i.e. here the contrast between official immigration policy, on the one hand, and the tactics of immigrants as actors, on the other hand, suggests that if the orientations, categorizations and perspectives of immigrants are always oriented towards the guidelines of the immigration authorities, the communication gambits of the immigration institutions themselves obviously also pick up categories and orientations of immigrants when they attempt to communicate with them about the immigration process:

> Are you interested in immigrating to Québec and working there? A typical immigration process based on the experiences of numerous immigrants is described below.
>
> (http://www.immigration-quebec.gouv.qc.ca/en/immigrer-installer/travailleurs-permanents/index.html, my emphasis – B. F.-J.)

The fact that direct relations between blogging immigrants and the institutionalized rules of immigration are developing can be seen in the fact that earlier immigrants from Latin America have now also founded semi-official information sites on the subject of immigration, for example Blog 11, which emerged from an association of Latin American immigrants and now passes on current official information to immigrants to Québec.

One of the earliest and most committed of the Latin American immigration bloggers, after his successful immigration, began to use his experience and excellent contacts in the Spanish-speaking blogger scene for his career and started his own business as an online consultant for questions of immigration from Latin America to Canada: Under the title *Ziegler Immigration Coaching*, he offers on his website not only a blog on current immigration issues (the original immigration blog has now been removed from the net), but also a comprehensive range of services related to immigration to Québec Within the community of blogging immigrants,[7] Guillermo Ziegler plays a very special role as a prototypical representative of his community. Almost all other bloggers refer explicitly to his blog or his website and link his websites in their blogs. Conversely, many blogs of Latin American immigrants to Canada receive a welcome greeting from Guillermo as the first commentary on their first posting, in which he acts as the mouthpiece of the immigrant blogosphere:

7 In fact, Latin American bloggers represent a stable and relatively coherent communication community that, with very few exceptions, does not involve immigrants from other regions of the world. Attempts to link further, in this case Francophone, immigration blogs to this community, as a French blogger tries to do with a comment to Blog 9 (Blog 9, commentary on the post of Sep. 10, 2007), are not successful.

Guillermo dijo…

Bienvenido al mundo del blogging, y al mundo de los inmigrantes a Canadá.

Te saludan "Los Ziegler...", desde Waterloo, ON

(Blog 14, June 18, 2007, Comment 1)

Guillermo said...

Welcome to the world of blogging, and the world of immigrants to Canada.

Greetings from "The Ziegler...," from Waterloo, ON

Guillermo a dit...

Bueno, que alegría ver que la gente tiene todo tan claro antes de llegar! Felicitaciones y ojalá

las cosas se te den así!

(Blog 8, Oct. 1, 2005, comment 1)

Guillermo said...

Well, what a joy to see that people have everything so clear before they arrive! Congratulations and hopefully things will turn out like this!

Guillermo dijo…

Hola Loquitos, bienvenidos al fascinante mundo de los blogs. Saludos desde Ottawa…

11 de junio de 2009

(Blog 3, June 11, 2009, comment 1)

Guillermo said...

Hello you loonies, welcome to the fascinating world of blogs. Greetings from Ottawa...

It emerges from these observations that the blogging immigrants, for their part, share orientations as a community and build constructions of meaning that enable them to develop their own concepts of identity within the given power structures of the immigration institutions. This will be examined in more detail in the following chapter.

3. The Appropriation of the Immigration Process: Meaning Constructions of Temporality by Immigrants

In their narrations and discussions, blogging immigrants gradually access each individual stage of immigration, interpret it, and finally attribute meaning to it for themselves, in a confrontation with the structures of the immigration process that initially seem inescapable to them.

To speak with Michel de Certeau, they behave like consumers of set types and systems because they use the immigration process in an almost subversive way for themselves and their very own needs, redefining and reinterpreting them.

What de Certeau describes using the example of the colonized Indians in Latin America therefore also applies to the Latin American immigrants to Québec, who deal in their blogs with the institutional constraints of immigration:

> Ainsi la réussite spectaculaire de la colonisation espagnole auprès des ethnies indiennes a été détournée par l'usage qui en était fait : même soumis, voire consentants, souvent les Indiens utilisaient les lois, les pratiques ou les représentations qui leur étaient imposés par la force ou par la séduction á d'autres fins que celles des conquérants ; ils en faisaient autre chose ; ils les subvertissaient du dedans – non pas en les repoussant ou en les transformant (cela arrivait aussi), mais par cent manières de les employer au service de règles, de coutumes ou de convictions étrangères á la colonisation qu'ils ne pouvaient fuir. Ils métaphorisaient l'ordre dominant. (de Certeau 1990, 54)

> Thus the spectacular victory of Spanish colonization over the indigenous Indian cultures was diverted from its intended aims by the use made of it: even when they were subjected, indeed even when they accepted their subjection, the Indians often used the laws, practices, and representations that were imposed on them by force or by fascination to ends other than those of their conquerors; they made

> something else out of them; they subverted them from within – not by rejecting them or by transforming them (though that occurred as well), but by many different ways of using them in the service of rules, customs or convictions foreign to the colonization which they could not escape. They metaphorized the dominant order: they made it function in another register. (de Certeau 1988, 32)

De Certeau is less interested in the power-subversion possibilities of these practices – which, in the case of our immigrants, are very small: Actually, they are completely absent, because the only real forms of rebellion against the laws of immigration would be the abandonment of the immigration project or the decision to enter illegally. Both, however, are topics that are not discussed at all in our blogs. Instead, de Certeau is interested in the identity-political content of the actors' tactics, their creative power to turn the irrevocable into something of their own that is inserted into their own identity. In contrast to strategy, which is based on a clearly power oriented calculation, tactics are a calculation that cannot count on some quality or feature of its own, certainly not with its own space and not with its own time structure. It is therefore also not in a position to define the "other as a visible totality." On the contrary:

> La tactique n'a pour lieu que celui de l'autre. Aussi doit-elle jouer avec le terrain qui lui est imposé tel que l'organise la loi d'une force étrangère. (de Certeau 1990, 60)

> The space of a tactic is the space of the other. Thus it must play on and with a terrain imposed on it and organized by the law of a foreign power. (de Certeau 1988, 37)

While strategy is "expansively" oriented towards the ever more progressive control of space and time, tactics always have to make do with an already predetermined order of space and time and are dependent on exploiting whatever gaps, openness and inconsistencies there are within this predetermined framework.

But as soon as we move our attention away from the power structures of official identity politics as de Certeau does, it becomes clear how creatively and resourcefully everyday actors, in our case immigrants, use, reinterpret, and exploit the given structures. What is important and entirely true for our object of investigation is the observation that this use of the existing structures, i.e. the tactics of the users, does not change the source structures themselves and that those who have the power to determine the structures cannot control their use and appropriation by the users.

This appropriation of directions given and their reinterpretation in the "tactical actions" of the blog entries forms the basis for the construction of a new group consciousness, the creation of an immigrant "we." The counterpart always already and principally addressed in the blogs, who only sporadically emerges from his virtuality as an interaction partner with his own contributions in commentaries, plays a role that should not be underestimated: it is the formal reason for the verbalization of experiences, thoughts, and feelings. This is, a division of labor, which at the same time enables reflection and abstraction through the epistemic power of writing (Raible 1999, 2004).

Now, what does this tactical appropriation of the existing structures look like in the case of the temporality structures of immigration in our corpus?

The objective of our first case study, in brief, is to describe in words and share with others the waiting period between two predefined stages of the immigration process, which was initially perceived as intolerable, then to reflect on it, and finally to creatively reinterpret the supposedly "senseless" waiting period into a period of reflection on the entire immigration process. The example ends with the realization, which represents the tangible and, above all, shared result of the reflection process, viz. that immigration is not just one episode among others in life, but a life-encompassing project. Let us now look at this process in detail, which serves as an excellent example of the "tactics" of the everyday consumer described above:

The first posting in Blog 12 of April 7, 2007 is entitled *Comienzo del cambio* ("Beginning of (the) change") and contains first hints at concepts of temporality: On the one hand, *comienzo* names the starting point of a process; on the other hand, the process itself in its function of bringing about change is perspectivized.

The following lines provide the context: the starting point of the blog simultaneously determines the beginning of an (obviously difficult) creative process (*crear un blog, crearlo* – to create a blog, create one) whose function is to comment on one's own experience during the immigration process to Québec:

> Después de muchos intentos fallidos de crear un blog, finalmente me he decidido a crearlo y comentar mi experiencia en el proceso de inmigración a Canadá-Quebec.
>
> (Blog 12, April 7, 2007)
>
> After many failed attempts to create a blog, I finally decided to create one and comment on my experience in the immigration process to Canada-Québec.

This is followed by an initial moment of reflection on temporality in the immigration process: by reflecting on the point in time at which she actually starts her blog, she determines that this point in time as the only correct one:

> Hubiese querido comenzarlo antes, pero bueno todo tiene su tiempo y es este instante el momento preciso para hacerlo.
>
> (*ibid.*)
>
> I would have liked to start it earlier, but well to everything there is a season and this is the precise moment to do it.

She justifies this determination with a pre-formed expression on the subject of time: "to everything there is a season." All the statements at the beginning of this blog come emphatically from the author's personal perspective ("I decided to create one," "my experience," "I would have liked"). Since authenticity and personal openness are among the generic characteristics of private blogs, this is not surprising:

> All weblog-related rules have one thing in common: whether it is the selection of other websites, comments on current topics or the presentation of everyday experiences and feelings, a weblog author is expected to communicate authentically and in "his own voice." This expectation of authenticity leads to online identities manifesting themselves in weblogs, which – as with personal homepages in general – are relatively closely linked to the real-world identities of the authors. (Schmidt 2005, 25, my translation – B. F.-J.)

It is therefore interesting that at the moment in which temporality becomes a theme, there is a conspicuous change into the impersonal: first the general saying, then an impersonal formulation in which time itself, namely the current point in time, becomes the subject: "this is the precise moment to do it."

The entirety of first blog entry deals meta-discursively with the beginning of the act of writing, which at the same time represents a specific point in time in the immigration process:

The chosen moment is that of waiting for the medical examination. It is therefore a time between Steps 4 and 5, in other words the period of waiting between two clearly pre-defined events, namely the receipt of the *Québec Selection Certificate* (CSQ, official step 4) and the request for an official medical examination, which is one of the conditions for applying for a permanent residence permit in Canada (step 5).

> En estos momentos estoy a la espera de las órdenes médicas, ha sido una espera interminable y nada que sé alguna noticia de la embajada.
>
> (Blog 12, April 7, 2007)

> At the moment I'm waiting for the medical examination, it's been an endless wait and I haven't even heard anything from the embassy.

Here the current blog writing process and the stage within the immigration process as described in the blog are narrowed down to one and the same moment. At the same time, the content of the following section is concerned with a temporally unlimited, endless stretch of time, a period of waiting, and thus an aspect of time that is institutionally regulated and, from the point of view of power and strategy, is an instance of temporality that cannot be influenced by her.

This blogger thus stages her own writing as a creative act that determines the meaning of the moment, the period between two stages of immigration, in this way resisting the infinity of waiting for the medical examination.

She can't change the length of the wait itself, but she can assign meaning to that time by selecting an exact moment within her wait to start her blogging activity. And so in her first entry she starts to reflect on her personal way of dealing with the tormenting time of waiting:

> Por otro lado, lo que puedo compartir en esta nota inicial es que he comprendido que todo tiene su razón de ser y este tiempo de espera me ha permitido cerrar varias cosas que tenía que dejar bien antes de irme del país, así como aprovechar el tiempo de estudiar francés, ahorrar y de empaparme un poco más de cómo es la vida en Montreal. Una de las cosas que he hecho es oír la radio quebécoise y leer la prensa tanto de Quebec como la de toda Canadá; es como hacerme la idea que vivo allá y estoy al tanto de lo que sucede.
>
> (*ibid.*)
>
> On the other hand, what I can share in this initial note is that I have understood that everything has its raison d'être and this waiting time has allowed me to make closure with several things that I had to leave behind me well before leaving the country, as well as take advantage of the time to study French, save and soak up a little more of what life is like in Montreal. One of the things I've done is listen to the Radio Quebécoise and read the press both in Québec and throughout Canada; it's like getting the idea that I live there and I'm aware of what's going on.

The blogger appropriates the waiting time by assigning it meaning, again with a pre-formed expression ("everything has its raison d'être"), namely the opportunity to prepare for the time after immigration, to familiarize herself with the other place and thus to arm herself for whatever may come in the future. The relevance of a message worth communicating ("what I can share") is assigned to this realization beforehand, which justifies its placement as the first blog entry.

The process of reflecting on the meaningfulness of the waiting time goes even further: the realization is raised in the final sentence in the first blog to a moral test and no longer affects herself alone, but all immigrants:

> Pienso que en este tiempo de espera se pone a prueba realmente nuestra fuerza de voluntad y determinación de seguir adelante con este proyecto de vida.
>
> (*ibid.*)
>
> I think that in this time of waiting our strength of will and determination to go ahead with this project of life is really being put to the test.

The process of making sense of the situation, triggered by the long waiting period, culminates in the idea that the immigration process is a life project.

The beginning of Blog 12 thus provides a good example of how a given time structure, which the blogger initially seems to be completely at the mercy of, is redefined by the epistemic power of writing and the interactive sharing of ideas: The useless waiting period, in which the immigration project does not seem to proceed, is reinterpreted and provided with meaning. As a moral test of staying power, the waiting period becomes quasi a new stage in the immigration process, one which is not institutionally defined, but all the more contributes to the formation of a common immigrant identity, the core of which is the definition of the immigration process as a life project.

The reinterpretation by the author of Blog 12 of the waiting time between two official steps on the path to immigration uses the gaps and openness of the institutionally given framework as a tactic in this way creating new contexts that contribute to the construction of a common immigrant identity. Such processes of reflection can be found in almost all the immigration blogs, and there is always an aspect of the perception and conception of time that seems to be specific to the situation of immigrants. Similar to the spatial "in-between" (cf. Bhabha 1994; 2000) of transnational migration movements, the time of immigration appears to be an in-between time, between a not-yet of the future and a no-longer of the past. This is a time in which the present appears to be oriented entirely towards future destinations and the view backward is limited to completed stages within the process of immigration, so that any reference to the current outside environment and its sense of time becomes more and more blurred. In this regard the author of Blog 4 writes in his post with the title "Entre tiempo" ("in between times"):

> Hace un mes que no escribo, y hace dos meses que entregamos los pasaportes para estampar la visa, realmente no ha sucedido nada relacionado con el proceso en sí. [...]
>
> Este tiempo ha sido bueno porque hemos podido reflexionar sobre las motivaciones que tenemos, por ejemplo, hace unas semanas me ofrecieron una mejor posición en la empresa, una posición que requiere un entrenamiento de al menos 8 meses antes de llegar a ser productivo, me ofrecieron un aumento, un mejor contrato y capacitación en herramientas sofisticadas, la verdad es tentador, pero ya sabemos lo que queremos.
>
> (Blog 4, Dec. 14, 2005)
>
> I haven't written in a month, and it's been two months since we delivered the passports to have them stamped with the visa, really nothing has happened related to the process itself. [...]
>
> This time has been good because we have been able to reflect on the motivations we have, for example, a few weeks ago I was offered a better position in the company, a position that requires training of at least 8 months before becoming productive, I was offered a raise, a better contract and training in sophisticated tools, the truth is that it is tempting, but we already know what we want.

Everyday events are evaluated in terms of their relation to immigration. In view of this, the time that the applicants for an immigration visa have just lived through is a waiting period that is used to reflect on their own attitudes to immigration. As a consequence, the attractive offer of a better paid job in the current workplace is conceptualized as an enticement ("tentador"), as a temptation that could lead the immigrant away from his actual path and is therefore not an option. The job offer is cited here by the blogger as a case study to show that even in the here-and-now only what has to do with reaching the goal of immigration has relevance. Following the same logic of temporal orientation, which is dedicated in its entirety to the perspective of immigration, Blog 4 as a whole is based on the concept of travel, which divides the perception of time into before, during, and after:

> Todas nuestras experiencias antes, durante y después de nuestro viaje a Quebec (Canadá). Este blog pretende servir como bitácora o diario de nuestro proceso de inmigración a Quebec. [...]
>
> (Blog 4, July 29, 2005)
>
> All our experiences before, during, and after our travel to Québec (Canada). This blog is intended to serve as a blog or diary of our process of immigration to Québec. [...]

The time of immigration is seen as a time of transition in which whatever is communicated is evaluated with regard to the immigration process and its goals. This means there is not just a personal sense of time of each individual blogger, but time also functions as a further element of the group identity of immigrants' blogosphere. This can be seen, among other things, in a comment on Blog 4. Here an immigrant from Venezuela intervenes to evaluate the immigration process as a laborious task in which reading immigration blogs functions as help and comfort:

> [...] soy de Venezuela y estoy junto con mi esposo en la ardua tarea de hacer el proceso para ver si nos dan la visa...y leerle ha sido un

> respiro, un aliento y a su vez un consuelo...exitos y suerte estimado Sr.
>
> (Blog 4, April 29, 2005, Comment)
>
> [...] I am from Venezuela and I am, together with my husband, in the arduous task of undertaking the process of seeing if we can get a visa...and reading it [Blog 4] has been a respite, a breath, and at the same time a consolation...lots of luck and success, my dear sir.

The transitional time is seen here as divided time which the bloggers live and suffer through together and in which their blogging is a service to the entire *Community of Practice.*

In some of our blogs, ones written from the perspective of completed immigration, the time "after," i.e. after reaching the destination, is described as a new parcours with new stages. Now, the goal is no longer immigration, but successful integration. Here too, as we have seen in the previous chapter, there are guidelines from the immigration authorities, namely *démarches* (courses of action) to be completed and *valeurs* (values) to be "learned."

As the following example shows, immigrants also create categories which describe integration in the country of destination and which they share with each other. But in contrast to immigration, they now orient themselves exclusively along the lines of their own experiences.

In a detailed comment on a posting in Blog 7, in which the author of the blog sets up a typology of Argentine immigrants in Québec (he distinguishes sixteen different types of immigrants), another immigrant confirms the validity of this typology for all Latin American immigrants:

> Muy bueno, ademas puedes facilmente cambiar argentino por venezolano o mexicano y funciona casi identico.
>
> No tuve ningun problema para identificar personas concretas de mi entorno que encajan cabalmente con cada uno de los esteretipos y yo mismo me vi reflejado en varios de ellos.
>
> (Blog 7, Nov. 29, 2006)

> Very good, you can easily change Argentinean to Venezuelan or Mexican and it works almost identically.
>
> I had no problem identifying specific people in my environment that fit perfectly with each of the stereotypes and I saw myself reflected in several of them.

As other commentaries confirming or supplementing the typology also show, these are valid collective attributions of identity in the community of blogging Latin American immigrants. Directly after the posting quoted above, the same blogger posted another text on the comment page. This one contains, as he himself admits, his attempt to divide the integration process experienced up to then into the time phases that all new immigrants pass through. These, in turn, were conceptualized as time structures collectively shared by the communication community:

> Difícil resumir en unas cuantas líneas los 31 meses desde que llegamos definitivamente a Canadá.
>
> Lo intentaré.
>
> Hay tres etapas muy claras que le suceden a casi todos los inmigrantes:
>
> (Blog 7, Nov. 29, 2005, Comment)
>
> It is difficult to summarize in a few lines the 31 months since we finally arrived in Canada.
>
> I will try.
>
> There are three very clear stages that almost all immigrants go through:

The three stages distinguished by this blogger do not now refer to any course of action officially prescribed by the immigration authorities, but to the subjective experiences of the new immigrants. The formulation uses indefinite "you" (Kluge 2012), which serves to generalize the whole:

> La primera es de euforia cuando acabas de llegar y todo te parece hermoso, diferente (y mucho mejor que en el pais de origen), interesante y crees que vas a encontrar fácilmente mil nuevas opciones positivas en tu futuro, es como si fuera una luna de miel con tu nuevo país (esa etapa te dura de 1 a 6 meses). [...]
>
> La segunda es de depresión, desencanto y un gran, gran estrés, es cuando vez que no todo es tan magnifico [...]
>
> La tercera es cuando logras una cierta estabilidad laboral, emocional y social, cuando empiezas realmente a integrarte a través de tu empleo, de tus vecinos, de tus nuevos amigos, de los compañeros de tu hijo, de sus actividades escolares y deportivas, cuando manejas mejor los idiomas y las expresiones locales, cuando obtienes mejores empleos, etc.
>
> (*ibid.*)

> The first one is of euphoria when you have just arrived and everything seems beautiful, different (and much better than in your country of origin), interesting and you think that you will easily find a thousand new, positive options in your future, it is as if it were a honeymoon with your new country (this stage lasts from 1 to 6 months). [...]
>
> The second is depression, disenchantment, and very, very great stress, it is when not everything is so magnificent [...]
>
> The third is when you achieve a certain stability in your job as well as emotionally and socially, when you really start to integrate in regard to your job, your neighbors, your new friends, your kid's classmates, their school and sports activities, when you master the languages and local expressions better, when you get better jobs, and so on.

The commentator establishes a temporal structuring of the integration process in emotional stages, and in doing so actually constructs a typology that is also accepted by other immigrants, as can be seen from its adoption by other bloggers: Blog 4 quotes the commentator's text literally, stating the origin of the quote, and comments on it under the title: "Stages in what happens to an immigrant:"

> Me parecieron muy buenas las etapas que describe [proper name] en otro blog, [...] sus comentarios que me parecen que son muy buenos y bastante parecidos a lo que nosotros pasamos y pensamos.
>
> (Blog 4, Jan. 15, 2007)
>
> I found very good the stages that [proper name] describes in another blog, [...] his comments, which I think are very good and quite similar to what we all go through and think.

Blog 4 receives 9 comments for this entry, almost all of which signal approval. Interestingly, the first comment comes from Guillermo Ziegler (cf. Chap. 2), the mouthpiece of the entire community:

> Guillermo dijo:
>
> 100% de acuerdo. Y creo que todos pasamos por esas etapas idefectiblemente.
>
> [proper name] dijo:
>
> Es muy bueno ese comment. Se encuentre trabajo rapido o no, todos pasan, problemas tenemos todos y los tiempos llegan.
>
> (Blog 4, Jan. 15, 2007, Comments 1 and 2):
>
> Guillermo said:
>
> I 100% agree. And I think we all went through those stages in an identical way.
>
> [proper name] said:
>
> That's a very good comment. Whether you find work fast or not, everyone passes, we all have problems and the times come.

Another commentator goes beyond the confirmation and emphasizes the supportive role that such reflections of the shared process play for each individual immigrant:

> Es muy agradable mirarse al espejo y reconocer en donde me encuentro situado como inmigrante. Sin duda sirve mucho hacer conciencia del proceso por el que uno pasa, pues esto facilita afontar los obstàculos con mayor efectividad.
>
> (Blog 4, Jan. 15, 2007, Comment 7, excerpt)
>
> It is very pleasant to look in the mirror and recognize where I am as an immigrant. Without a doubt, it is very useful to be aware of the process one goes through, because this makes it easier to overcome obstacles more effectively.

These examples reveal the activities of the blogging immigrants to be successful tactics which help to process the personal experiences and the emotions that trigger them. They share them with others and thus create common processes of reflection that help them to come to terms with the various obstacles they are faced with. At the same time, the shared experiences and reflections create an identity as a community of blogging Latin American immigrants.

4. Narrations of the Immigration Process

A broad interdisciplinary research tradition of sociologists, psychologists, and linguists has for several years been devoted to the investigation of identity construction in narratives (Quasthoff 2001; McAdams 2006; Lucius-Hoene and Deppermann 2002, 2004a). Narration is understood as an essential element in the social construction of reality:

> It is widely accepted that narratives are a fundamental means through which people make sense of and share their take on experiences, no matter how big or small, how life-changing or insignificant. (Baynham and De Fina 2017, 31)

This applies in particular to identity constructions in special "problematic situations" (see Chapter 1) such as immigration processes.

Within the tactics that concern the temporality of immigration narratives have a special relevance, because temporality is a central element of the reconstructive achievements of narration:

> Narrative interpretations presuppose [...] temporal expansion and create it at the same time. Understanding a memory as a memory (and distinguishing it from a present sensory impression as past, which is an important goal in trauma therapy) is based on the awareness of the past as the past, which in turn is only possible if there is also an awareness of the present as the present. (Brockmeier 2015, 7, my translation – B. F.-J.)

In order to be able to narrate something, I must be able to assign meaning to the story. However, the story only acquires this meaning in retrospect, from the distance made possible in a present that looks back:

> Retrospection is an essential component of human temporality, of being in time. It manifests itself in a delay or shift, a postponement of meaning and significance to a later point in time, precisely when we can look back and give meaning to things. (Freeman 2015, 14; my translation – B. F.-J.)

While in direct experience it is a logical principle that an earlier event cannot be influenced by a later one, this is not the case with a narrated event, because the reconstructed meaning of the event narrated is formed by the end, from the overall plot of the story:

> Indeed, it is an inherent and intractable feature of how we remember and continually restory our pasts, shifting the relative significance of different events for whom we have become, discovering connections we had previously been unaware of, repositioning ourselves and others in our networks of relationships. The past is not set in stone, but the meaning of events and experiences is constantly being reframed within the contexts of our current and ongoing lives [...]. (Mishler 2009, 36)

In our immigration blogs, in addition to the plot of the story narrated, we must always reckon with the goal of the *parcours*, immigration, or, in the phase after immigration, integration as a meaningful end of the story narrated. This results in a double temporal orientation in the narrative reconstructions in our immigration blogs in which meaning is attributed under the influence of the end. In many narratives, this double orientation becomes directly recognizable in the doubling of the "coda" of narration (Labov and Waletzky 1973): in a first interpretation this refers to the event narrated and in a second interpretation, to its significance for the chain of events that make up the entire process of immigration.

In the immigration blogs, the path traveled is traced in individual narratives, whereby the authority to interpret events passes from the institution that dictates the path and its temporal structures to the narrator, who can narrate the individual stages as authentically experienced and ascribe meaning to this experience within the context of his or her life. In this way, the entire process of immigration as a part of the individual's own experience can be gradually shaped narratively and can thus also be processed interactively. In this respect, narration offers blogging immigrants a particularly important tactic which enables them to adopt the given path and attribute meaning to it.

4.1 Narrative Appropriation of the Temporal Structures of Immigration

All narrative blog entries are by definition reconstructive, since narration is a reconstructive process. This gives all narrations a double temporal structure: the time of the narrated event vs. the time of the narrative. For our question about temporality structures as tactics of immigrant actors, the historical reality of the narrative is of less interest than the way of the blogger narrate in order to gain access to the construction process of narrative structures,

> which is pragmatic-interactive and motivated by the current interests of self-enquiry, self-assertion and self-representation. (Lucius-Hoene 2000; my translation – B. F.-J.)

In what follows the focus is on the elements of temporality that can be discerned in the narrative reconstructions of bloggers.

As is suggested by its format of blogs they are oriented along the lines of a diary or logbook. As a result, most blogs are created in continuous acts of writing that tell a story shortly after it was experienced. In this way, the readers follow the narrated path of immigration step by step. Since the bloggers accompany their narratives with comments, they reveal which step of the process they are currently at. However, there are also some immigration blogs that start only after arrival in the country of destination. Some of them do not narrate everyday life immediately as it is currently experienced, but instead narratively reproduce the entire immigration process that has taken place up to that point. And even though these blogs also take individual stages and experiences out of the process and present them as particularly worthy of narration, the chronological sequence of events is adhered to in the macrostructure of the blog.

For the readers of such a blog who have not followed the entire writing process chronologically, but rather start off directly with the narration of a particular event, the temporal location of these narratives in relation to the time of blogging remains unclear: the standardized presentation of the postings in reverse chronological order means that the current posting appears at the very top, so that the reader who has not been constantly following the course of the blog cannot grasp the larger textual context without deliberate effort. The reader of these blogs, which often cover particularly large temporal stretches between narratives, is therefore often unaware that the events narrated occurred far back in the past; for, as a rule, individual entries and thus also individual narratives in the blogs are dated only according to the time of the narration and not according to the time of the narrated stories. It can therefore happen that the time structure of the narrative construction of a blog entry is explicitly negotiated, as in the following example:

Following the story of his wife's first job interview in Canada, the author of the post received the following query from a reader in the comments section:

> P.D. esto que cuentas está pasando o es pasado?
>
> (Blog 1, June 2009, comment)
>
> P.S. This that you tell is it happening or did it happen in the past?

The narrator replies:

> Es del primer mes de estadia aqui es decir entre Marzo-Abril del 2008... saludos y gracias
>
> (*ibid.*)
>
> It is from the first month of the stage then namely in March or April of 2008 ... Best wishes and thanks

The fundamental difference between the narrative reconstruction of immediate experience and the tactic of constructing the narrations from the total perspective of a much later time lies above all in the more far-reaching reflection and the interpretative possibilities that the view of the entire process of immigration in greater hindsight permits. This is also evident from the fact that these narratives are accompanied by evaluative commentaries that include an interpretative positioning of the narrative in the overall process of immigration:

Thus, Blog 1 reports on the blogger's very first days after arriving in Canada at a distance of more than a year. The individual narrative posts are repeatedly interrupted or completed by retrospective evaluations of the narrated actions and perceptions:

> La primera noche en Montreal.....
>
> [...]
>
> Aquel 15 de marzo lo recordare siempre, pues vi mi primera nevada caer, nada grande, pues el invierno estaba en sus finales, pero aun nos acompañaría hasta abril. Sin embargo fue mágico ser bien recibidos, sentirnos acogidos, comer bien y luego llegar a dormir nuestra primera noche oficial en Montreal. No se porque pero en ese momento me sentí tranquilo. **Era como si el examen hubiera comenzado y el hueco del estomago se cerro súbitamente**. [...]
>
> Hoy, mirando hacia atrás, **no cambiaria ninguna de mis decisiones a la llegada**
>
> (Blog 1, April 9, 2009, my emphasis in bold, B. F.-J.)
>
> My first night in Montreal.....
>
> [...]
>
> I will always remember that March 15th, because I saw my first snow falling, nothing big, because winter was at its end, but it would still be with us until April. However, it was magical to be welcomed, to feel welcomed, to eat well and then to sleep our first official night in Montreal. I don't know why, but at that moment I felt tranquil. **It was as if the examination had begun and the cavity of my stomach had suddenly closed**. [...]
>
> Today, looking back, **I wouldn't change anything about my decision to go there**.

In this way, subjective perceptions and feelings which are narrated take on new meaning and interpretations, in this case in comparison with an exam situation, a comparison that only becomes possible after the fact at a distance. The concentrated tranquility experienced earlier as inappropriate and difficult to understand, despite all the imponderabilities of the situation, appears to be justified from the point of view of the long since passed exam (viz. successful acclimatization to the new environment). Only the knowledge that one has already successfully completed the further steps towards integration makes a positive evaluation of these first perceptions, feelings, and experiences and the resulting actions possible. Only then can a deeper meaning be ascribed to the emotions experienced.

4.2 Narrations of Stages and the Collective History of Immigration

In the context of immigration blogs, attributing a special meaning to a situation experienced in the immigration process and shaping it to make it "worth telling" (Quasthoff 1980; Lucius-Hoene and Deppermann 2004b) also always means categorizing it in some way as typical of the immigration process. Its narrative value is thus directly related to the identity-constructing functions of the blogs for the entire community. An effective means of guaranteeing worthwhile narratives lies in the selection of narratively well shaped events: Within our corpus it can be said that it is always the same type of situation that is narrated by the blogging immigrants. These are situations that are defined by the official *parcours* and therefore have to be lived through by every immigrant.

As we have already seen (chapters 2 and 3), these recurring situations include significant steps within the path to immigration, such as the waiting period before being invited to the medical examination or the official medical examination itself (more on this in chapter 5), arrival in Canada, the first conversation in French in Québec, or the search for accommodations, etc.

One of the events that are regularly narrated is the selection interview at the Canadian Embassy. This stage is particularly challenging for Latin American immigrants, both in terms of content (it is important to prove that you are well prepared for life in the country of destination and that you meet all the requirements) and in linguistic terms (the entire interview is conducted in French, so that it is also a test of your linguistic skills). The following example of one woman's narration is presented in its entirety in order to show the diversity of the narrative techniques used:

> La entrevista
>
> Bueno no hay blog de inmigrantes sin pasar por el concebido relato de la entrevista.
>
> Algo que quiero recordarle a las personas que aun no han comenzado su proceso, es que es inútil contratar una agencia o abogado para que los represente. Los trámites son sencillos: llenar formularios y juntar certificados (que de todas maneras uno mismo debe solicitar).
>
> Nos avisaron la fecha de la entrevista con dos meses de anticipación. Todo este tiempo nos sirvió de preparación. Teniamos que justificar nuestro deseo de establecernos en Québec, ojo con esto, no se trata de decir lo mal que estamos en Colombia y lo lindo que se ve Canada en las fotos, se trata de ir a contarle a un consejero el porqué de esta elección, porqué Québec?
>
> Pues bien, iba en que tuvimos suficiente tiempo para prepararnos. Yo, siendo la aplicante principal, estaba extra-nerviosa. Todo debido a que? Pues hacía algunos meses había solicitado la visa de turismo española para ir a visitar a mi tio favorito en todo el mundo. Yo continuaba repitiendome: "Si me negaron una visa de turismo, como carajos voy a obtener una residencia permanente a un país que no he visitado?"
>
> Afortunadamente, teniamos a un conocido en Québec quien nos escribió algunas palabras tranquilizantes, entre otras y algo que es lógico y uno olvida, que el gobierno canadiense contrariamente al español, tiene una politica de puertas abiertas a la inmigración.
>
> En lo que más nos ayudó: poderlo escuchar hablar francés "quebecuá" la mayoria de los inmigrantes estudiamos francés standard. Todo esto me devolvió la confianza, la fe y hasta el sueño. Fue un lindo gesto de su parte, tomarse la molestia de hablar un ratito con

nosotros, unos desconocidos prácticamente, y tan solo a unos cuantos dias de la entrevista, parecía más bien algun ángelito caido del cielo.

Llegado el gran día partimos en viaje hacia Bogotá. Llegamos un día antes para no lucir tan cansados luego de diez horas de viaje. Pasamos nuestro dia hablando en francés, repitiendo mil veces las respuestas de nuestra entrevista "ejemplo."

La cita era a las 14 h. Salimos a las 12 h para evitar cualquier trancón bogotano. Llegamos a las 12 h 45. Almorzaremos cerca a la embajada! Pensamos ingenuamente... Nos bajamos del taxi y de una nos fuimos a la embajada... estaba cerrada, claro. Nos fuimos al centro comercial que queda justo en frente... No logramos almorzar! Era un manojo de nervios espantoso, yo sentía que no tenía estómago, solo un nudo en su lugar... Él, jefe de familia con nervios de acero, calmaba sus angustias dandome ánimo. Decidimos no pensar en nada y solo ver las vitrinas mientras pasaba el tiempo... Además nos veiamos muy lindos en nuestros trajes... como si fueramos los ejecutivos más importantes que merodeaban por ahi cogidos de la mano...

13 h 45 Nos dirigimos hacia la embajada. Esperamos pacientemente a que abrieran. Llegó el recepcionista, nos anunciamos y nos hizo esperar unos momentos... llamó a un señor del que no recuerdo nada, sólo que era muy amable y nos dijo: Tenemos que ir al hotel que está frente a la embajada, ya que al señor consul no le gustó el lugar... "Qué????" -pensé yo- "ese tipo tiene que ser jodidisimo!!!" Nos intercambiamos una mirada de confusión mezclada con terror con mi marido... De vuelta al centro comercial donde habiamos pasado una hora dando vueltas...

Llegamos al lobby del hotel. Los celadores nos remarcaban mucho. Vienen a la entrevista de inmigración, no?

- Ajá (Que nos delataría?)

- Ya los anunciamos.

Nos requisaron, pero no a nuestro guía ya que el se la pasa en eso todo el día “escoltando” a los candidatos de un lado de la calle al otro. Inútil hacerlo pasar por tanta molestia...

A mi me requisó una mujer. Muy amable.

- Tienes nervios?

- Muchos.

- Tranquila les va ir bien.

- Gracias!

Luego al ascensor. El nudo en mi estómago no se quería desatar... siempre con las manos agarradas esta vez con mucha fuerza, como pasandonos ánimo, asi en un lazo indestructible...

Minutos eternos de espera en el pasillo esperando a que Mr. “Terrible” Abriera la puerta... Por fin la abrió:

- Buenas tardes doctor, (dijo el guía)

- Buenos días (contesta Mr. Terrible)

Qué!!! habla español??? Pensabamos nosotros (que alivio).

- Acá están los candidatos, hasta luego!

- Ok (Contesta Mr. Terrible)

- Bonjour!

- Bonjour Monsieur (contestamos al unísono)

Nos dimos cuenta que probablemente “Buenos días” sería lo único en español que le escucharíamos, y así fue.

Pues bueno luego de las presentaciones y sentarnos comenzó la entrevista. Todo salió diferente a como lo pensabamos pero fue para bien, Mr Terrible se presentó y pude dejar de pensar en él como si fuera una especie de ogro, en realidad era todo lo contrario, un señor muy comprensivo y paciente, comenzó hablandonos como a niños pequeños y a medida que veia que comprendíamos todo, la cosa se animó y comenzó a hablar rápido... muy rápido.

Las personas somos increíbles. Llevabamos 40 minutos de entrevista y estabamos los tres muy a gusto, incluso ya en confianza, como si fuesemos amigos de toda la vida. Mi pregunta indiscreta:

- Qu'est-ce que vous dérange de l'Ambassade?

- Le bruit!!! Il y a des bâtiments en construction juste a côté... on peut rien entendre!!

Y tenía razón. Al lado de la embajada estan construyendo dos edificios... nunca pensamos en eso! Que malpensados siempre pensando lo peor!!!

Y asi terminaba nuestra entrevista... El consúl nos felicitó incluso nos abrazó, dijo que nunca nos olvidaria, nosotros, conmovidos casi hasta las lágrimas, tanto esfuerzo y preparación se resumió allí, nunca esperamos que todo nos saliera así de maravilloso....

"Vous avez très bien réussi, bravo! Soyez bienvenus à votre nouveau pays"

No salimos caminando... salimos volando! Un nuevo capitulo de nuestras vidas comenzaría, ese 18 de septiembre de 2007. Nosotros nunca lo olvidaremos "non plus monsieur [family name]"

(Blog 13, March 1, 2009)

The interview

Well, there's no immigrant blog that doesn't go through the idea related to the interview.

One thing I want to remind people of who have not yet begun their process is that it is useless to hire an agency or lawyer to represent them. The procedures are simple: fill out forms and collect certificates (which you must request anyway on your own).

We were informed of the date of the interview two months in advance. All this time served as preparation. We had to justify our wish to settle in Québec, be careful with this, it's not about saying how bad we have it in Colombia and how nice Canada looks in the photos, it's about telling a counselor why this choice, why Québec?

Well, we had enough time to prepare. Me, being the main applicant, I was extra-nervous. All because of what? A few months ago I had applied for a Spanish tourist visa to visit my favorite uncle anywhere in the world. I kept repeating: "If I was denied a tourist visa, how the dickens am I going to get a permanent visa for a country I have never visited?"

Fortunately, we had an acquaintance in Québec who wrote us some reassuring words, among other things and something that is logical and one forgets, that the Canadian government, contrary to the Spain, has an open-door policy on immigration.

What helped us most: being able to hear him speak "Québec" French; most immigrants study standard French. All this gave me back my confidence, my faith and even my dream. It was a nice gesture on his part, to take the trouble to talk for a little while with us, practically strangers to him, and only a few days before the interview, he seemed more like some angel who had fallen from the sky.

When the big day came, we left on the trip to Bogota. We arrived a day early to not look so tired after ten hours of travel. We spent the day speaking French, repeating a thousand times the responses from our "example" interview.

The appointment was at 2 p.m. We left at 12 o'clock to avoid any possible Bogota traffic jam. We arrived at 12:45. We would have lunch near the embassy! We thought naively... We got out of the taxi and one of us went to the embassy... it was closed, of course. We went to the shopping center that was right in front of us... We couldn't have lunch! We were a terrible bunch of nerves, I felt like.... He, head of the family with nerves of steel, calmed his anxiety by encouraging me. We decided not to think about anything and only to see the showcases while waiting for the time to pass... We also looked very handsome in our suits... as if we were the most important executives who were prowling around holding hands...

1:45 p.m. We headed for the embassy. We waited patiently for them to open. The receptionist arrived, we introduced ourselves and he made us wait a few moments... he called a gentleman who I do not remember anything about, only that he was very kind and he said to us: We have to go to the hotel that is in front of the embassy, since his honor, the consul, did not like the place... "What????" – I thought, "That guy's got to be screwed up!" I exchanged a look of confusion mixed with terror with my husband... Back to the mall where we had spent an hour circling around...

We arrived at the hotel lobby. The guards easily recognized us. They are coming for the immigration interview, aren't they?

- Uh-huh (Would he tell on us?)

- We already announced them.

We were searched, but not our guide since he spends all day "escorting" the candidates from one side of the street to the other. It is useless to make him go through so much trouble...

A woman searched me. Very friendly.

- Are you nervous?

- Very.

- Don't worry, everything'll be fine.

- Thank you!

Then to the elevator. The knot in my stomach didn't want to be untied... always with my hands clasped this time with a lot of strength, as if passing on courage to us, as in an indestructible bond...

Eternal minutes of waiting in the corridor waiting for Mr. "Terrible" to open the door... At last he opened it:

- Buenas tardes, doctor, (said the guide)

- Buenos días (replied Mr. Terrible)

What! Does he speak Spanish??? We thought (what a relief).

- Acá están los candidatos, hasta luego [Here are the applicants, good bye]!

- Okay (Mr. Terrible replied)

- Bonjour!

- Bonjour Monsieur (we answer in unison)

> We realized that "Buenos días" would probably be the only Spanish we would hear from him, and so it was.
>
> Well, after the presentations and sitting down, the interview began. Everything was different than we had thought but it went really well. Mr Terrible introduced himself and I could stop thinking about him as if he was some kind of ogre, in fact he was quite the opposite, a very understanding and patient gentleman, he started talking to us like little children and as he saw that we understood everything, it all became more lively and he started to talk fast... very fast.
>
> People are incredible. We had been interviewing for 40 minutes and the three of us were very comfortable even in confidence, as if we were lifelong friends. My indiscreet question:
>
> - What bothers you about the embassy?
>
> - The noise! There is a building site right outside … you can't hear anything!
>
> And he was right. Next to the embassy they are constructing two buildings... we never thought of that! What a bad idea to always assume the worst!
>
> And that was the end of our interview... The consul even congratulated us with a hug, said that he would never forget us, we, we were moved almost to tears, so much effort and preparation was bound up in this that we never expected that everything would turn out so wonderfully.....
>
> "You have been very successful, bravo! Welcome to your new country."
>
> We didn't walk out... we flew out! A new chapter in our lives would begin on September 18, 2007. We will never ever forget "Monsieur [family name]."

The structure of this post very nicely follows the normal form of oral narratives as presented by Labov and Waletzky in 1973 (cf. also Kallmeyer 1981): It begins with an "orientation" that categorizes the following narration as an obligatory element of immigration blogs:

> Bueno no hay blog de inmigrantes sin pasar por el concebido relato de la entrevista.
>
> Well, there's no immigrant blog that doesn't go through the idea related to the interview.

At the same time, the blogger refers here to the constructedness ("concebido") of the post. And although she proceeds in strictly chronological fashion in the following, it is above all the different speeds of narration and the targeted use of narrative procedures that show that the post was carefully designed.

> The actors portrayed have not simply acted as they were narrated as doing, but it is the narrator himself who makes them appear in a certain way, who selects, shapes, correlates, and interprets their earlier utterances and actions as they finally appear as elements of the narrative. (Lucius-Hoene and Deppermann 2004a, 175)

Before the actual narrative begins, the blogger inserts a fundamental remark that is explicitly addressed to immigration novices and has the format of a piece of advice. She wants to stress that engaging an agency or a lawyer is not really helpful in the immigration process, since all the essential steps have to be applied for and completed in writing, but, in any case, personally by each immigrant him- or herself.

The relation of this advice to the following narrative remains unclear for the time being. Only at the end does it become clear that the narrative can be regarded as an illustration of the "on your own" from this general advice, namely in the following argumentation: Only if you have prepared for the exam situation independently and experienced it yourself, are you in a position to gain insights from such experiences which strengthen your own personality in such a way that the entire immigration process can be successful.

This is followed by giving the beginning of the story a temporal orientation (the couple had two months to prepare for the interview). The fact that the more precise circumstances and conditions of the embassy interview did not have to be specified here is explained by the initial reference to the obligatory character of this narrative: all immigrant blogs tell about this central stage on the path whose conditions and requirements, it can be assumed, are known in the immigrant community.

The main part of the narrative (the complication at the embassy) gradually builds up an arc of tension with a special time structure: First, the two months of preparation are reported on at length, then the narrative time narrows its focus and briefly describes the day before the interview. Then the time narrows even more and reports on the hour before the interview, the last quarter of an hour, and the minutes before the beginning of the interview. In ever more extensive detail, situational elements and the associated subjective feelings – fears and imagined scenes, which in turn trigger nervousness, etc. – become more and more apparent. This conveys to the reader the ever-increasing nervousness and fear, which is also described in strong images ("a terrible bunch of nerves," "I didn't have a stomach, only a knot where it was"). Further details describe strategies for coping with the growing nervousness (abandonment of the project to eat lunch, holding hands, distracting themselves, etc.). Shortly before the actual interview is related, the blogger switches to dramatic narrative mode to describe the encounter with the embassy staff. This increases the tension even more. At the same time, the reader experiences the time of the narrative as if in real time.

At this point of the highest tension a retarding moment occurs: A member of the embassy leads her out of the embassy again, since the interview is to take place in the hotel opposite at the request of the consul. Here the reader gets an insight into the fantasies of the immigrants, who imagine the consul is a monster ("ogre") because of this inexplicable action ("That guy's got to be screwed up!").

The beginning of the actual interview is then quoted again in direct speech ("Bonjour! – Bonjour Monsieur (we answer in unison)").

At this point, the tension abruptly leaves off. The rest of the interview with the consul (which, according to the blogger, lasts 40 minutes in all) is considerably reduced and reported on in just a few lines. Only to illustrate how relaxed and friendly the interview was, at the end of the interview, does the speaker switch back to direct speech: The blogger even dares at this point to ask the consul what bothered him about the embassy (as he had moved the interview to the hotel opposite); and his explanation that it was too loud for him there because of a construction site is received with relief as a banal, rationally justified decision.

At this point the blogger inserts an "evaluation" which refers to the fears described above and sees her own behavior as wrong: "What a bad idea to always assume the worst!" By formulating here the lesson that she herself drew directly from what she had experienced during the interview, she passes it on to her readers as a first attribution of meaning to and interpretation of what she had experienced at the actual time of the event reported.

As a "resolution" of the narrative, the success of the interview is shown narratively by describing the embrace of the consul at the end and quoting his congratulations on passing the test and welcoming them to their new homeland:

> Vous avez très bien réussi, bravo! Soyez bienvenus à votre nouveau pays
>
> (*ibid.*)
>
> You have been very successful, bravo! Welcome to your new country

The post ends with a "coda" that perspectivizes the events in regard to the blogger's present situation and once again explicitly emphasizes the relevance of this stage for the immigration process:

> Un nuevo capitulo de nuestras vidas comenzaría, ese 18 de septiembre de 2007. Nosotros nunca lo olvidaremos "non plus monsieur [family name]"
>
> (*ibid.*)
>
> A new chapter in our lives would begin on September 18, 2007. We will never ever forget "Monsieur [family name]."

We recognize here the double time structure of the constructions of meaning mentioned above: For in contrast to the "evaluation", the narrative is attributed meaningful relevance here on the second level, the level of the entire immigration process.

By using various narrative techniques such as scenic interactive re-enactments, the representation of imagined possibilities of alternative courses of action, the rendition of emotions (nervousness, fears, anxiety, and relief), or the deliberate build-up of tension through the alternation of descriptions of actions undertaken, direct speech renditions, descriptions of subjective feelings, and comments from the current narrator's perspective, the blogger succeeds here in constructing her personal version of the new well-known and repeatedly told event. She describes herself and her husband as exemplary immigrants who have meticulously and competently prepared themselves for the challenge of interview and are therefore in a position to master it despite their great nervousness. She also describes herself and her husband as persons who have matured in a successfully completed stage of self-knowledge.

The collective significance of their narration for the community as a whole becomes clear in some comments posted by readers. This is what the author of Blog 1 writes in his commentary:

> Chevere...me alegro mucho de tu experiencia....salir de esa entrevista es "descansador"....adelante...duro con el frances...esa es la llave! aqui...cualquier minuto que estudien de mas...sera un minuto de menos sin trabajo!
>
> Saludos y felicidades de nuevo.
>
> (Blog 13, March 2, 2009, Comment)

> Cool...I'm very happy with your experience....to get out of that interview is "restorative"...go ahead...hard with the French...that's the key! here...any minute you study more...it'll be a minute less without work!
>
> Greetings and congratulations again.

As an immigrant who has already gone through this stage himself, he is in a position to confirm the emotional attributions of the narration. At the same time, he points to a topic that has been treated only marginally here, but which is of particular importance for the community, the problem of immigrants' mastery of French. – In fact, the narrative presents the French language competence of the immigrant couple as very good, which is an exception within our corpus.

Another anonymous commentator writes:

> Muy lindo relato realmente se me pusieron los ojos sollozos, cuanta emocion, realmente estoy contando los dias para poder pasar la entrevista.
>
> (Blog 13, March 17, 2009, Comment 1)
>
> Very nice story really got my eyes tearing up, how much emotion, I'm really counting the days till I am able to pass the interview.

This immigrant apparently finds himself in his *parcours* before the stage told here. Above all, it is his emotional participation that is relevant, allowing him to adjust to the stage inwardly even before he goes through it.

Our corpus contains numerous narrations of this stage. And each time, similar to this case, they are extensively discussed in commentaries. In this way, the individual history of the progress of immigration from stage to stage becomes a chain of narratives that connect the blogs and their readers with each other, forming a dynamic network of the stages that are recounted over and over again, something which develops within the static structure of the officially given *parcours*.

As an element of the identity of the blogger community, this network represents a concept of temporality in which immigration appears as an eternally repeated sequence of the same stages, which is simultaneously lived through again and again in new and individual ways. The author of Blog 1 expresses this as follows:

> Pienso que todo esta dicho y cuando lo pienso, me doy cuenta de que esta dicho de miles de formas, pero todas diferentes. Eso es la inmigración. Millones de ópticas sobre un mismo tema, todas validas, todas veraces, todas falsas a la vez.
>
> (Blog 1, November 13, 2011)
>
> I think that everything is said and when I think about it, I realize that it is said in thousands of ways, but all different. That's immigration. Millions of views on the same subject, all valid, all truthful, all false at the same time.

A much more concise, condensed form of narration is presented in the next example. As we have already seen in Chapter 2, the waiting time between two stages is a frequent reason for posts. The immigrant can only actively continue his way again when the institution, for instance the immigration authorities or the Canadian embassy, issues an official request to do so. The waiting period must therefore be filled with activities (e.g. preparatory language courses, research on the target region, etc.) or reflections relating to your own situation now or in the future. While most bloggers use these interim periods for reflections, the author of Blog 14 chooses a narration for this.

Blog 14 starts in one of these waiting times with his very first post, which is entitled "The wait ..." Although what follows has a narrative format (strongly oriented toward spontaneous oral narrative) – note above all the use of the tenses, the strict chronological structure marked by discourse markers such as "*bueno pues* [*well*]" and the use of time adverbs and dates – it is strictly speaking merely a list of the stages completed so far, each with briefly inserted ironic comments (set in italics below) and a concluding "moral:"

> Bueno pues en agosto de 2006 recibí mi CSQ (Certificat de Selection du Québec) y en noviembre envié mis papeles a la embajada de Canadá para todo el trámite federal.

Bueno pues hace un mes me llegó un sobrecito de la embajada dándome instrucciones de donde ir a hacerme los exámenes médicos y los analisis policiales.

Hace dos semanas que entregué los papeles y bueno, *ya saben como son en las embajadas, te tratan con la punta del pié. Lo peor es que esos monos son mexicanos!!!; en fin...*

Sin embargo en el documento me pedían --además de los exámenes policiales en México-- ir a hacerme la toma de huellas a una oficina de policia en Canadá, *cosa que se me hizo medio raro. Aunque estuve viviendo un tiempo en Montreal, no estuve más de seis meses.*

Envié un correo a la Embajada y estoy en espera que me contesten.

Si no tengo que ir, pues solo restará esperar....

(Blog 14, June 14, 2007)

Well, in August 2006 I received my CSQ (Certificat de Selection du Québec) and in November I sent my papers to the Canadian embassy for the whole federal process.

Well, a month ago I received a small envelope from the embassy giving me instructions on where to go for my medical examination and police reports.

It's been two weeks since I delivered the papers and well, *you know how they are in the embassies, they step on you with their feet. The worst thing is that those monkeys are Mexican!*

However, in the document they asked me – in addition to the police examinations in Mexico – to go and have my fingerprints taken at a police office in Canada, *something that was a bit strange for me. Although I lived in Montreal for a while, I didn't stay more than six months.*

I sent an e-mail to the Embassy and I am waiting for an answer.

If I don't have to go, then all that remains is to wait....

The macrostructure of this "narration" is reminiscent of the lists of the stages of immigration given with their dates, as described above (cf. Chap. 2). In this case, the waiting time for the last stage before possible immigration is used for a kind of narrative recapitulation of the stages already completed, which at the same time provides a quick orientation about the blogger himself in the opening part of the blog. In the blogger's brief comments, however, the subjective feelings triggered by the experiences can also be seen and in this way are offered to the community as possible interpretations. This is how his anger about the degrading treatment in the embassy is made relevant, or about the insecurity triggered by the conditions imposed by the Canadian police. The two comments on this contribution therefore also deal with the representation of subjective feelings in the posting.

4.3 Putting Narrative into Perspective, Positioning and Constructing a Collective Identity

In the example just presented, one can see that the way in which the processes and stages that are narrated are put into perspective reveals the blogger's specific individual interpretation of what he or she has lived through. The irreverent, spontaneous style as well as the direct address of the readers ("ya saben [you know]") in the commentary and the contemptuous remarks on the behavior of the embassy representatives or the resigned conclusion that shows passive waiting as the only option, all these very subjective ways of putting the processes into perspective emphasize the immigrants' helplessness and powerlessness in the face of the arbitrariness of institutions. If we compare this depiction of the *parcours* traced with the tabular enumerations already presented, we can see how large the creative scope of the bloggers' narratives actually is.

Among the narrative procedures used by immigrants as tactics of the appropriation of and ways of coping with the immigration process these are, above all, the tactics of self-positioning and of positioning others (Lucius-Hoene and Deppermann 2004a; 2008). These allow bloggers to characterize themselves and the others as actors in the narrated event in a particular way and thus attribute certain characteristics, abilities, and attitudes to them:

> In the narration of self-experience, the narrator must identify him- or herself as the agent of the story, [...] as an actor shaped by experience. He or she must stage their past narrative ego with particular characteristics and modes of action and shape this self-revelation while taking into account listener- and situation-related aspects. (Lucius-Hoene and Deppermann 2004a, 167)

The selection of the events to be told from the multitude of possible stations on the route is just as important as the way in which events are contextualized or the narrative format is chosen. All these narrative procedures contribute to the creation of a narrative identity:

> In general, positioning refers first and foremost to the discursive practices by means of which people create and represent themselves and others in verbal interactions in relation to one another as persons, which attributes, roles, qualities, and motives they claim and ascribe with their actions, which in turn are functional for the local representation of identity in conversation. (Lucius-Hoene and Deppermann 2004a, 168)

A comprehensive analysis of the positioning techniques in narrations from our corpus alone would easily fill a complete book. For this reason we can only look at a small selection of examples which, above all, show a relation to concepts of temporality and explore the tactical scope available to immigrants in their narrations in order to develop concepts of temporality in connection with the immigration process. The tactics of positioning are never exclusively about identity work for the single individual who constructs the narration, but always about a contribution to the identity of Latin American immigrants to Québec as a community.

In the following example, the blogger narrates an event that took place shortly after his arrival in Québec.

> Mi primera cita a entrevista.....
>
> Un día cualquiera de la semana venia yo, ya ni se de donde, en el autobús [...]. Una vibración "cellular" me saco de mis pensamientos de inimmigrante para introducirme en el mundo de las conversaciones imposibles de autobús. Los que han recibido una llamada en francés quebeco en un bus a menos de 45 días de haber llegado a Montreal, sabrán de que hablo!...para quienes no saben, he aquí el bosquejo contextual:
>
> (Blog 1, July 1, 2009)
>
> My first interview appointment....
>
> Once on one week-day or the other I was coming, I don't even know where from, on the bus [...]. A "cellular" vibration took me out of my immigrant thoughts to enter the world of impossible bus conversations. Anyone who has received a call in Québec French on a bus less than 45 days after arriving in Montreal will know what I am talking about!...for those who do not know, here is a sketch of the situation:

This blogger chooses a narrative attitude that emphasizes his reconstructive achievement by clearly recognizably selecting from the contextual information that which is relevant to his narrative line (or at least information that is not irrelevant: "I don't even know where from") and by assigning his perceptions and thoughts to categories typical of his social roles ("my immigrant thoughts") and his situation ("impossible bus conversations"). In addition, he addresses an imagined readership that is categorized as having experienced exactly the same thing. At the same time, this provides him with a further opportunity to position himself as someone who was completely overwhelmed by the situation and its linguistic demands. For the further course of the event, the blogger uses dramatization techniques by reproducing the telephone conversation literally as it happened. In addition to using paraverbal devices (e.g. dots to reproduce pauses, question marks to represent non-understanding, capitalization to indicate the intensity of the sounds), he adds numerous comments, in parentheses, on the speech he reproduces in the form of direct address of the imagined reader. The comments on this post contain explanations of the context and, above all, repeated invitations for the readers to put themselves in the narrated situation. This creates a kind of complicity with the knowing reader, who should also share the emotions of the protagonist:

> BZZZZZ…………BZZZZZZZZZ…….BZZZZZZZZZZ (a ver imaginación POR FAVOR!!!! Es la vibración del celu!)
>
> YO: Oui, alo?
>
> VOZ : M. [proper name]? (a ver ...imaginación POR FAVOR!!!! Obviamente la persona sabia mi nombre!)
>
> YO: Oui, c'est moi à l'appareil....
>
> VOZ: M. [proper name], mon nom est Km ????? yen, j travaille pour Rlf C H????? on v…chr…lle….car… reçu tr…Rsumé…intesnt ….pour la position qu'on cherch…on aimrai…vous rncntrer…le plus tôt possbl si vs et encr à l rchrch….est-ce que vs est encr n chrch d l'emploi
>
> YO: ehhh, mmmm…..a veeerrrrrr….bueeeno….si claro… (de aquí en adelante mis palabras en español para facilitar la comprensión…pero como dije antes todo transcurrió en francés).
>
> VOZ: Vous v conisz RLF C????....on est ste a lost d lile….est-ce que l ## d'abrl à ??? hrs c'est beau pr vu?
>
> YO: ehhhhh….mmmmm…perdoneme pero hay mucho ruido y no escucho muy bien…me podria repetir, por favor?
>
> VOZ: est-ce que l ## d'abrl à ??? hrs c'est beau pr vu?.....not addrs est ??????????? autrt ???????
>
> Quelle heure vous-va bien?????
>
> YO: mmmmm…….si…si claro a esa hora estaria bien….
>
> VOZ: 9:00 ça vous va?
>
> YO: (pensando para mis adentros: o sea que lo que habia entendido no era la hora….ah veo!) si si ….esta perfecto!
>
> VOZ: vs vs avz ntz bien toutes nos informations? (traduccion: "tiene usted claro TODOS LOS DATOS QUE NECESITA?")

Y es aquí donde no se porque, para que, con que objeto, que fin buscaba…nunca me lo explique!!!!! Pero a pesar de haber comprendido menos del 2% de la información excluyendo obviamente que era para una entrevista que me llamaban, respondi de la manera en que mis nervios crispados, manos temblorosas, frente sudorosa y cerebro bloqueado me aconsejaron:

YO: Oui! Merci!

VOZ: Ok M. [proper name]…..bonne journeé…..au plaisir de vous rencontrer.

YO: Oui, oui….merci…

En resumen: no supe quien me llamo a una entrevista para no se que puesto en no se cual empresa y yo acepte ir a no se donde sin saber cuando…pero eso si……….la cita era a las 9:00 a.m.!!!!!

Sin embargo, me sentí feliz…era mi primera cita a entrevista!!!!!

(Blog 1, July 1, 2009)

BZZZZZZZZZBZZZZZZZ............ BZZZZZZZZZZZZZZZZZZZ (Imagination PLEASE!!!!!!! It is the vibration of my mobile!)

Me: Yes, hello?

VOICE: Mr. [proper name]? (Imagination PLEASE!!!!!!! Obviously the person knew my name!)

Me: Yes, it's me speaking......

VOICE: Mr.[proper name], my name is Km ??????yen, I work for Rlf C H?????? we ar...look...you...because...received very...application...interest...for the position we are looking for...we would like to meet you...the soonest possible if you are still search...are you still looking …job

Me: ehhhh, mmmm.......lets seeeeeeeeeeeeee....okayyyyyyyy....yes of course... (from now on my words in Spanish to facilitate comprehension...but as I said before everything happened in French).

VOICE: Do you know RLF C?????....... we are loc… in the east of th.. isle....does the ## of aprl suit you???

Me: ehhhhh....mmmmmmm...excuse me but there's a lot of noise and I can't hear very well...could you repeat for me, please?

VOICE: does the ## of aprl at???o'clock suit you?..... our addrs is ?????????. highway???????

What time would suit you?????

Me: mmmmm....... yes... yes okay that time would be fine....

VOICE: 9:00 that would be okay?

Me: (thinking to myself: or what if what I had understood was not the time....ah I see!) yes ....it's perfect!

VOICE: vs vs avz ntz bien toutes nos informations [yuh, yuh 'ave noted all our information down]? (translation: "Do you have all the information you need?")?

And this is where I don't know why for what reason, with what object, what purpose I was looking... never explain it to me!!!!!! But in spite of having understood less than 2% of the information excepting, obviously, that it was for an interview that they called me, I answered in the way in which my twitchy nerves, trembling hands, sweaty forehead and blocked brain advised me:

Me: Oui! Merci!

VOICE: Ok Mr. [proper name].....have a nice day.... a pleasure to meet you.

Me: yes, yes… thank you...

In short: I didn't know who called me for an interview so I don't know which company and I agreed to go I don't know where without knowing when......but nevertheless ....the appointment was at 9:00 a.m.!!!!!!

However, I felt happy...it was my first appointment for an interview!

The blogger shares with his readers a particularly stressful situation here, which he cannot cope with due to his lack of language skills and the unfavorable conditions (telephoning with a mobile phone during a bus trip). At the same time, however, he presents himself here as a person who does not give up even in difficult situations, who despite the impossibility of success brings conversation to an end. In the concluding "evaluation" he explicitly categorizes his reactions as failures, but nevertheless comes to a positive overall assessment of what he has experienced. This attribution of meaning can only take place in relation to his process of integration as a whole: He seems to have succeeded in receiving an invitation to an interview for a job. In fact, as his readers know, he is writing his narration in the situation of having a secure job that he has meanwhile gotten. So one of the functions of this narration is precisely that, to frame the actual significance of this failure in the long-term process. For the readership, the central message of the evaluation is to have a positive attitude in spite of failure ("However, I felt happy").

In the next example, too, a negative experience is narrative in such a way that a positive attribution of meaning can take place with regard to the process of integration:

Blog 4 begins about a year after immigration and tells about integration in Canadian everyday life. On-going events are usually told either on the same day or a few days later: In the following example, the blogger tells how she had to wait five hours with her slightly injured son in the emergency room of a clinic until he was finally treated. Interwoven with the narration there are explanatory and evaluative commentaries that take into account different imagined perspectives: the perspective of an Argentine middle-class woman, the perspective of a Québec woman, and finally her own, which unites the two previous perspectives and is also an expert perspective, since the blogger is a nurse. In this way she positions herself as someone who has different standards of evaluation and can adjust these competently to the appropriate contexts:

> La guardia del hospital
>
> Por un accidente doméstico, nada grave, pero que necesitaba una ida al hospital para suturar una cortada de Lucas en el tobillo estuvimos 5 horas en la guardia.

Para todo argentino de clase media esto de pasarse 5 horas en la guardia del hospital es una total barbaridad (salvo para el pobre argentino que frecuentaba los hospitales de la zona oeste del gran Bs As donde esta espera era muy común). Para el quebecoise pasar todo el día en la guadia es normal y hasta tiene su lógica y te dan toda una serie de explicaciones al respecto.
En honor a la verdad, sí es mucha espera y su lógica tendría que reducirse a 2 hs de espera en un día normal, pero la verdad es que faltan médicos y no saben (o las Ordres no quieren)resolverlo. De todas maneras, me pareció muy bien el "Triage"que es un sistema de clasificación de la gravedad que hace el enfermero de triage y que atiende muy rápido a toda la gente y los manda a rayos, laboratorio,ect y los "entretiene" según el caso y luego a esperar de acuerdo a tu gravedad. [...]
Esto que cuento parece de terror, pero como enfermera que soy, creo que tiene su lógica para que la gente sea atendida con equidad (que no es lo mismo que igualdad). [...]
Al final, Lucas recibió 3 puntitos de manos de una doctora muy amable y a casita!

(Blog 4, July 19, 2006)

The outpatient clinic

For a domestic accident, nothing serious, but one which required a trip to the hospital to suture a cut Lucas had in his ankle, we spent five hours in the outpatient clinic.
For all middle-class Argentines spending 5 hours like this in the hospital outpatient clinic is a total barbarity (except for poor Argentinians who frequent the hospitals in the western area of greater Buenos Aires, where such waiting is very common). For a Québec woman to spend the whole day in the hospital is normal and even has a logic of its own and everybody gives you a series of explanations on the matter.
To be honest, it is a lot of waiting and it would have to be reduced to 2 hours of waiting in a normal day, but the truth is that there are not enough doctors and they don't know how to solve it (or the people in charge don't want to). In any case, I was very happy with

> the "triage" which is a system of classification according to the seriousness of the injury that the triage nurse decides on and that takes care of everyone very quickly and sends them to radiology, the laboratory, etc. and "sorts them out" according to the case and then has them wait depending on how serious your case is. [...] This story seems terrifying, but as a nurse, I think it has its logic for people to be treated with fairness (which is not the same as equality). [...] In the end, Lucas got three little stitches from a very nice doctor!

The blogger contextualizes the long wait with background information by explicitly noting the rationality of the event ("has a logic of its own") and by referring to the system of triage practiced in Canadian emergency rooms as a logical justification of the long waiting time. In her explanation of the long waiting time in the outpatient clinic, the blogger thus positions herself as a multiple expert, both as a professionally experienced nurse and as an everyday expert both in Argentina and in Québec. She thus automatically assumes a mediating role vis-à-vis her readers (who are thus categorized as immigrants still in Argentina or ones on their way to Canada). In the final evaluation, she emphasizes the principle of "fairness" (*equidad*; French *equité*) attributed to the triage process, a quality that is official in Québec society, as described, for example, in the following official communiqué:

> [...] the fundamental values of Québec society, namely equity, social justice and solidarity.
>
> (http://www.midi.gouv.qc.ca/fr/ministere/enonce-valeurs.html)

In this way, the blogger succeeds in reinterpreting an inherently negative experience with the outpatient reception system of Canadian clinics and identifying it with a positive value that allows the immigrant community to attribute meaning to the entire narrative in the context of successful integration ("learn the values of Québec").

For people who are in an earlier stage of the *parcours* such narratives by bloggers who have completed the immigration process successfully engender a special conception of time and structure of temporality. In a comment on the blog entry just quoted, one of her followers writes:

> Hola:
>
> Mi nombre es [proper name] y hace unos meses he seguido con bastante interés su blog, me ha atrapado su forma de narrar su vida en [name of town] y las cosas que cada día cuentan; actualmente estoy tramitando mis papeles para inmigrar a Canadá y precisamente el lugar que he elegido para vivir es [name of town]; el motivo principal de este mensaje es para preguntarle sobre la vida cotidiana de ese lugar, he investigado en las paginas oficiales pero creo que me falta el testimonio de alguien que ya este inmerso en la cotidianidad. Me gustaria saber la facilidad o dificultad que hay para encontrar vivienda y trabajo [...] cualquier cosa que me quisieran contar , sugerir u opinar sobre el dia a dia de los habitantes de [name of town].
>
> De antemano, muchas gracias por la información y **averiguaré cada día un poco más de la vida en [name of town] a través de su blog.**
>
> (Blog 4, commentary of July 20, 2006 at 5:30, my emphasis)
>
> Hello:
>
> My name is [proper name] and I followed your blog for several months now with a lot of interest, you have fascinated me with your way of narrating your life in [name of town] and the things you tell every day; I am currently working on my papers to immigrate to Canada and precisely the place I have chosen to live is [name of town]; the main reason for this message is to ask you about daily life there, I have researched in the official pages but I think what I'm missing is the testimony of someone who is already immersed in everyday life. I would like to know how easy or difficult it is to find housing and work [...] anything they would like to tell me, suggest or give an opinion on about the daily life of the people living in [name of town].

> Thank you very much in advance for the information **and I will find out every day a little more about life in** [name of town] **through your blog.**

Here it becomes clear that those who are still on the path of immigration have been given a share in a life they are trying to imagine through these narratives from Québec. At the same time, the narratives offer them ascriptions of meaning that they confirm in their comments. From the point of view of temporality, this means that the narrative reconstructions of past experiences of the already successfully immigrants become possible projected experiences in the future. Plans for the future combine with reconstructions of actual experiences and make possible the concretization of their own visions, but also the learning of mechanisms of adaptation (e.g. changes in attitudes and expectations), even before the corresponding situations themselves are experienced.

Positioning procedures in narrations and related interpretations of experiences during the immigration process open up for these readers new perspectives, concretizations, and details for their own projections regarding the immigration path. In this way, the reconstructed past of some becomes the basis for the projected future of others.

4.4 Narrations on the Experience of Temporality in Immigration

One of the narrative procedures that concerns concepts of temporality is the description of time as it is experienced during the immigration process, namely as other, distorted, and shifted in relation to usual, everyday time and this works in both directions:

As we have seen (cf. chapters 1 and 2), in the personal experience of immigrants, the focus is above all on holding out BETWEEN two stages. Since applicants for a visa cannot determine the duration of this interim period themselves, it is important to position themselves in relation to the fundamental openness of the waiting period that must be endured. This conceptual work of attributing meaning to the waiting period is a topic in each of our immigration blogs. And usually the blogger's own perception of time is also described:

In the vast majority of cases, as we have already seen in some examples, the waiting time is experienced as infinitely long and stressful. For example in Blog 1:

> La espera de esas fechas fue una pereza....todos los dias ansiando el famoso sobre color reciclaje..todos los dias viendo que se acababa el tiempo para nuestro cronograma inicial....todos los dias pasaban como si fueran 6 meses cada uno de ellos.
>
> (Blog 1, March 6, 2009)
>
> The wait for those appointments was full of lethargy....every day marked by longing for the famous recycled colored envelope...every day seeing that the time in our initial schedule was running out....every day passed as if it were 6 months long, each one of them.

In the narration of the waiting time for the invitation to the medical examination, both the impatience of the immigrants in view of the elapsing time (and their original schedule) becomes visible, as does the weariness of the daily waiting, so that a single day appears like six months.

The temporal interval between two stages thus manifests itself as a distortion of the perception of time. The background to this distortion is the perception that the normal everyday time of the here-and-now in the country of origin appears to be suspended, seems to be irrelevant compared to a projected time to be reached ("our initial schedule").

In the further course of the same post, this blogger now describes the moment when this waiting comes to an end, when the intermediate time dissolves and the next stage of the course is heralded since the request for a medical examination has finally arrived:

> De pronto en un dia de esos en los que la espera se te habia amodorrado de tanto soñar despierto con los planes que tenia...llegue a mi casa y lo encontre encima de mi cama....asi nada mas....como si nunca lo hubiera estado esperando, con esa sencillez de sobre de carta postal que no va a servir para nada, pero guardando la llave de nuestro viaje.
>
> (Blog 1, March 6 2009)

> Suddenly on one of those days on which the wait had been one of drowsy day-dreaming of the plans I had....I arrived at my house and found it on my bed....just like that....as if I had never been waiting for it, with the simplicity of a postcard that is not going to be useful for anything, yet holding the key to our trip.

The narration makes clear how strongly the immigrant's subjective perception of time is linked to the external events that are imposed on him by the immigration authorities. It shows that the possibility of beginning a new stage, like an unpredictable and, despite the long, tense expectation appears ultimately as a ridiculously banal event which comes into one's life and changes everything. The everyday time in the blogger's home country, in which he still finds himself in the narrated time, seems to be completely excluded from his perception, as if unreal: what has been urgently expected for weeks seems downright unreal at the moment of arrival, "as if I had never been waiting for it." At the end of this narration, in which the completion of the medical examination is only briefly reported, the perspective is directed entirely and exclusively towards the projected emigration:

> Cansados pero con el deber cumplido nos fuimos a mi casa a hablar y planear lo que pensabamos que en menos de un mes y medio estariamos comenzado, nos fuimos a hablar de nuestro viaje....por enesima vez!
>
> (*ibid.*)

> Tired but with duty fulfilled we went to my house to talk and plan what we thought, that in less than a month and a half we would be on the go, we went to talk about our trip .... for the umpteenth time!

In numerous narratives in our blogs, a similar temporal orientation of the immigrants becomes visible, one which is directed exclusively towards projections of the future. The waiting time between two stages fades out. In its place come drafts of a future time in which the focus is on further stages and their themes, which themselves are painted in detail as scenes in the imagination. This is what Blog 8 says:

> Como aún no nos entrgan la visa, hemos aprovechado esta temporada navideña y cuasi-vacacional, **para reflexionar y plantearnos los diversos escenarios** en los cuales nos podemos desenvolver.
>
> (Blog 8, Jan. 10 2006, my emphasis)
>
> Since we have not yet been given a visa, we have taken advantage of this Christmas and quasi-holiday season **to reflect on and consider the various scenarios** in which we can develop further.

Under the title "La 'sweet' wait" (sic!) Blog 1 tells in a post about the waiting time directly before departure:

> No era fácil concentrarse, no era un ejercicio sencillo separar la cabeza del futuro para traerla al presente y hacernos, de paso, olvidar ese hueco en el estomago. No era fácil vivir el día a día, pero era la única forma de vivir más rápidamente el mañana.
>
> (Blog 1, March 10, 2009)
>
> It was not easy to concentrate, it was not a simple exercise to separate our heads from the future and bring it to the present and make us forget that hole in our stomachs. It was not easy to live day by day, but it was the only way to live tomorrow more quickly.

In the face of the excitement of being so close to the desired departure, the everyday life of the present becomes a distraction from the actual goal on which the emigrant must concentrate in order to move forward day by day. At the same time, this distraction serves to make waiting bearable.

All these examples reveal the perspective which the waiting time imposed on immigrants due to external constraints (usually waiting for the immigration authorities to issue decisions) in the first phase of immigration. The time before moving to the country of destination is a time of waiting in which the present gradually becomes blurred and concentration turns entirely to the future in the country of destination.

A completely different way of perceiving time is described in narratives that deal with the first period of time after arrival in Canada. All of a sudden, events, experiences, and impressions crowd together so closely that it seems almost impossible to cope with them in time that passes far too quickly. This is how the author of Blog 1 describes it in the narration of the first months in Montreal under the title "De como se vive un siglo en un mes..." ["How you live a century in a month..."]):

> Nuestros días parecían siglos y al completar un mes y medio sentiamos haber vivido casi un año aquí.
>
> (Blog 1, May 27, 2009)
>
> Our days seemed like centuries and after a month and a half we felt we had lived here almost a year.

Here the time seems to be condensed so that the numerous impressions can no longer be processed:

> Pero cada día era una nueva etapa.... [...] tantas historias...tantas palabras....tantos conceptos tantas cosas nuevas día a día......
>
> (*ibid.*)
>
> But each day was a new stage.... [...] so many stories... so many words....so many concepts so many new things from day to day.......

Immediately after immigration, the present appears to be the only real factor in the perception of immigrants. This, however, now takes place faster than the individual impressions and experiences can be processed and mastered. There is no longer any talk here of further plans for the future and even less of the past, the path that has been successfully mastered so far.

All in all, the narratives of the blogging immigrants show numerous new concepts of temporality that distinguish the group of immigrants from their surroundings in their home country or country of destination, assigning them a status that differs in their own – speeded up as well as stretched out perceptions of time. The time before entering Québec is always directed solely at what is yet to come; it is designed in preparation and these designs increasingly also determine everyday perception. One can categorize this typical concept of time before departure, as some of the immigrants themselves do, as an intermediate time, a not-yet and not-anymore, that becomes graspable again and again in the narratives and represents an essential element of the shared identity.

The image of immigration as an endlessly repeated *parcours* emerges above all from the narration of the same routes and milestones in each new immigration blog. In numerous posts it is discussed that the process of immigration is an infinitely repetitive one, which has to be experienced and lived through anew each time:

This brings us to the burdens and difficulties that the immigrants address in their posts and which they try to process and overcome by writing their posts and comments.

5. Blogging about the Immigration Process as a Therapeutic Coping Strategy

In his analysis of the use of tense in natural languages, which is still highly relevant for both text linguistics and literary studies, Harald Weinrich (1964) uses numerous examples to demonstrate that tense is not directly related to the representation of temporality in individual languages. Rather, the grammatical category of tense as a linguistic universal belongs to the means whose function of expression is directly related to the speech situation in the interaction:

> In regard to tense the language shows the same persistence as with the [the category of] person. Therefore, if our considerations are correct, language will have just as strong, "vital" reasons to take tense seriously and not to dispense with it. We also derive from the analogy to the person of the verb the assumption that the tenses of the verb may also have to do with the most elementary, but also the most fundamental layer of language, layer where communication is at stake. The lifeblood of language must also be in the tenses. The tenses of language must have something to do with the speech situation in which language and the world meet. (Weinrich 1964, 25; my translation – B. F.-J.)

According to Weinrich, a central function of tense is to express the fundamental attitude of the speaker towards what has been said (the "world"). This can be shaped in two ways, namely as a discussed world for which the speaker assumes a certain responsibility:

> Here the world is not narrated, but *discussed*. The speaker is engaged; he has to act and react, and his speech is one piece of action that changes the world a little, but at the same time obliges the speaker a little. (Weinrich 1964, 50; my translation – B. F.-J.)

Or as a narrated world in which the speaker is free to create his own interpretation of what he has experienced:

> It is irrelevant to the character of a narrative qua narrative whether the story is true or fictional. It is also irrelevant whether it is unpretentious or literarily stylized. In the end it doesn't matter what genre rules it obeys in detail. [...] Narrative is a characteristic behavior of man. We can relate to the world by narrating it. (Weinrich 1964, 49; my translation – B. F.-J.)

If we look at the therapeutic functions and accomplishments of immigration blogs in the following, we can see that they use the tactics of processing and coping with difficult experiences in both of the linguistic forms of tense that we find in the immigration blogs. However, while there is already an extensive tradition of research on the healing powers of the narrative mode, this is not the case to the same extent for the mode of the discussed world.

We start with the narrative mode and link it up directly with the examples in the preceding chapter. In the research on coping with difficult life situations, stressful experiences or traumas, narration has so far been highlighted as being therapeutically effective. Numerous studies from psychotherapy, narrative psychology, clinical conversational linguistics, and narrative medicine (Charon 2008) have shown that people who suffer from the effects of stressful or even traumatizing situations experience a healing effect in narration, i.e. in the narrative reconstruction of these experiences and the methods used to structure them – and in particular in the narrative location of the experiences within the chronological sequence of their own biography:

> The verbalization of stressful memories is of great importance in the treatment of trauma disorder. Finding words for stressful experiences serves the purpose of coping with them; and in the interpersonal context this also brings relief. In addition, verbalization fulfils a meaningful and explanatory function. In the course of the processing of a traumatic event, a narrative is gradually developed that encompasses what has happened and a person's own reactions to it and gives the stressful experience a place in that individual's life

> story. If this reconstruction succeeds, the trauma is processed. (Sack 2015, 150; my translation – B. F.-J.)

This healing effect of narration can be explained in various ways. From a linguistic point of view, Weinrich states that the tense of narration allows us to take a position on what we have experienced and felt and so to "relate to the world" and to communicate our attitude to others and negotiate about it with them. As a structural system that functions according to collectively valid rules, it is language, in the first place, which makes it possible to share inner feelings and states of being (Bühler 1934). At the same time, the mode of narration, as we have seen in Chapter 4, allows us to position ourselves and thus attribute to ourselves those qualities and attitudes that we feel are positive elements of our identity or perhaps ones we aspire to. Perhaps the most important achievement of narration in this context is that it shapes, in a creative process, what we experience, that it gives structure to the experience itself. Compared to direct experience, narrated experience has passed through the filter of consciousness, which leaves out much and adds something:

> For all narrated time is condensed time. Every instance of condensation [...] is selection, and every selection is interpretation. We are a far distance from physical time! (Weinrich 1964, 57; my translation – B. F.-J.)

It is precisely the narrative design of experiences that enables blogging immigrants as well as trauma patients to reproduce what has happened to them, but reconstructing it in such a way that it corresponds to their current interpretation and the idea they want to convey of themselves. Through this filtering process, the perspective of the narrative simultaneously creates a safe distance, both a distance to the narrated experience and also a distance to the emotions associated with it:

> The horror of the narrated event obviously does not affect or hardly affects the situation, which as a narrative situation has in principle eased the tension. The terrible events, even if they are only one day

> old, are filtered through the narrative and mitigated to a considerable extent. (Weinrich 1964, 49f; my translation – B. F.-J.)

From the point of view of memory research, the most important achievement of retelling, that is, narrating, stressful experiences is the potential for change in the memory content through associative additions and targeted reconstructions. Memories which originate in situations that triggered a particularly high degree fear or stress may therefore only be stored fragmentarily and not transferred to the long-term memory. By embedding a fragmentarily stored experience in a rational structure, e.g. in the chronological processes of the narrator's own biography and anchoring it to the existing content of long-term memory, the experience so narrated can be newly constructed and in this way integrated into the content of some other part of long-term memory (Sack 2015, 151f).

The so-called narrative exposure therapy (Schauer, Neuner, and Elbert 2005; Neuner, Schauer, and Elbert 2009) makes particular use of this integrative capacity of narration. This finds substantiation in the fact that a person traumatized in the clinical sense is initially unable to tell a story:

> [This person] has not yet escaped from the traumatic scene; in the literal sense, no extraction has taken place. Instead, the person is him- or herself the trauma. A spatial location and temporal historicization has not taken place. (Neuner, Schauer, and Elbert 2009, 303; my translation – B. F.-J.)

In the narrative exposure therapy founded by psychologists in Constance and Bielefeld, people suffering from post-traumatic stress syndrome are specifically encouraged to tell their biographies under guidance (Schauer, Neuner, and Elbert 2005):

> Narrative exposure therapy is based on the recognition that successful trauma therapy ultimately requires the correction of memory pathology. Only when the free-floating fragmentary images, sounds, and feelings are placed in the spatial and temporal context of the person's biography can the trauma be remembered as a story and

> not as a present threat. The therapist is present as a committed and sensitive listener who actively helps to put into words the most gruesome details of memory and to convert them into an understandable chronological narrative. (Catani and Neuner 2020, 29; my translation – B. F.-J.)

What has a healing effect on trauma patients also has a therapeutic effect on immigrants who find themselves exposed to the unalterable structures of the institutionalized process of immigration and who are repeatedly exposed to situations of psychological stress in various stages of this process.

For the blogging immigrants, too, the main function of therapeutically effective narration is the successful integration into their own life history of experiences that are difficult to process and in this way to create the basis for conceiving them within an generally coherent context of identity:

> The narrativization of the traumatic experience and its integration into a historical, socio-cultural, and auto-biographical context serve the purposes of appropriating and integrating what has been heterogeneously experienced. By embedding the experience of trauma in one's own history of experience, it is implicitly or explicitly provided with meaning for one's own biography and identity. [...] In connection with this, personal values and convictions, normative ideas, and belief systems often achieve thematic centrality. This can make it easier for them to be evaluated and given a contour within the experience of trauma or loss and thereby affirmed or rejected. The attribution of meaning thus also makes it possible to convey important aspects of identity. (Scheidt and Lucius-Hoene 2015, 27; my translation – B. F.-J.)

As we have seen in the past chapters, the identity-building achievement of narration in the immigration blogs is not only related to the writer himself, but affects the entire community. Imagined and real readers serve the bloggers as necessary counterparts, people whose existence is the very reason for the narrative processing of one's own experience. Their regularly posted comments confirm, supplement, and encourage the bloggers and thus also play an important role in the processing of difficult experiences. In contrast to the therapist, however, the authors of the commentaries are themselves directly involved in the immigration process. They also share the subjective feelings that accompany the experiences; in other words: they are literally sharing the suffering.

Our first example of the healing power of the narration of burdensome experiences comes exceptionally from a French blog. It serves as a kind of foil for the following example from the Latin American blog corpus. Both posts tell the story of the obligatory medical examination, one of the stages in the immigration process which is regularly presented in immigration blogs. The narrative reconstruction of this stage, which all immigrants have to go through, highlights, especially in blogs of French immigrants, that the examinations are perceived as exhausting, expensive, and also humiliating (Frank-Job and Kluge 2012, 60ff). One way of narrating this experience and at the same time coping with it is to use irony and sarcasm. This is the case in a blog from a French immigrant who wanted to emigrate to Québec with his wife and two small children:

> C'est le 27 juillet 2004 que toute la famille a eu rendez-vous pour la visite médicale chez le Dr [proper name]. Voiçi donc le déroulement de notre journée…
>
> Nous arrivons donc à 14h [name of street], à coté des Champs-Elysées. Nous y sommes restés 1h30 pour 2 adultes 1 enfant et 1bébé de 22 mois.
> C'est [proper name, my wife] qui s'y colle la première, euh!!! avec [name child1], car quand une certaine distance le sépare de sa mère, une "alarme" naturelle se déclenche.

Puis c'eusse été au tour de [name child 2], no problemo, et enfin mon tour, qui fût torché en à peine 10mn. Nous voiçi donc alléger de 250€

Passage à la Radiologie. Après avoir remonté les Champs-Elysées sous le soleil, à vitesse assez rapide, à pied, en pouss pouss pour le petit dernier (veinard!!) et accompagné des "moins vite, j'ai mal aux jambs" que notre pauvre petite puce nous implorait. Nous arrivons juste à l'heure, nos 2 radios ont été faites en 15mn maxi. Et tac! 70€

En route pour le laboratoire d'analyses.

On commence par [child 2] pour l'examen d'urine, [my wife] reste à ses cotés 10mn dans les toilettes.........en vain, puis vient mon tour, prise de sang (qu'il est beau le plafond au dessus de la chaise du patient à qui on prélève du sang!!!), puis examen d'urine.

Vient au tour de [name child1], no problemo. On retente alors pour [name child 2], à mon tour de rester 10mn dans les toilettes à ses cotés...toujours rien.

L'heure tourne, comment faire? bon, nous optons pour une escapade au fast food du coin pour gouter (accompagné de 50cl d'eau pour la puce). Après 20mn de promenade sur les Champs, nous retournons au labo. [My wife] réessaye pendant que je calme [name child1] dont l'alarme s'est déclenchée. Au miracle, ma fille reviens heureuse d'avoir rempli de 3 gouttes son bocal. « Bon!! ça ira! » nous a répondu l'assistante médicale. coût 91,53€

Enfin, nous retournons dans notre véhicule, pour enfin arriver 1h15 plus tard dans notre "home sweet home." Et là, vous ne devinerez jamais, ma fille sort de la voiture en pliant les jambs "papa vite, je veux faire pipi"!!!!!

(French Blog, July 31, 2005)

Medical check-up

It was on July 27, 2004 that the whole family had an appointment for the medical examination at [proper name]'s home. So here is the progress of our day....

We arrive at 2pm [name of street], next to the Champs-Elysées. We stayed there for an hour and 30 minutes for 2 adults, 1 child and 1 baby of 22 months.

It is [my wife], who goes through it first, uh!!!! with [child no. 1], because when a certain distance separates him from his mother, a natural "alarm" is triggered.

Then it was the turn of [child no. 2], no problem, and finally it's my turn, which was knocked off in just 10 minutes. So we are now relieved of 250€

On to Radiology. After going up the Champs-Elysées under the hot sun, at a fairly fast speed, on foot, pushing the little one (lucky!!!) and accompanied by moans of "slower, my leg hurts" that our other poor little flea was imploring us with. We arrive just on time, our 2 x-rays were made in 15 minutes max. And pow! €70

On the way to the laboratory for the specimen analysis.

We start with [child no. 2] for the specimen, [child no. 1] stays at [my wife's] side 10 min. in the rest room............. in vain, then comes my turn, blood sample (how beautiful the ceiling is above the chair of the patient whose blood is drawn!!!!), then specimen examination.

Next comes [child no. 1], no problem. We then try again with [child no. 2], now my turn to stay 10 minutes in the rest room next to [child no. 2] ... still nothing.

> The clock is ticking, what can we do? Well, we opt for a getaway to the local fast food joint for a feast (including half a liter of water for the flea). After a 20-minute walk on the Champs, we return to the lab. [Child no. 2] tries again while I calm down [child no. 1], whose alarm has not gone off. Miraculously, my daughter comes back happy to have filled her jar with 3 drops. “All right!! It’s okay!” replied the medical assistant. Fee: €91.53
>
> Finally, we return to our vehicle, to finally arrive an hour and a quarter later at our “home sweet home.” And then you’ll never guess, my daughter gets out of the car while crossing her legs
>
> 
>
> “Daddy, fast, I gotta pee”!!!!!!!

The linguistic format chosen here (narrative in the present tense, division into sections separated by time and type of investigation, enumeration of costs, comic-ironic commentaries) gives the reader a direct insight into the events in their chronological sequence and at the same time allows the staging of what has been experienced as a collectively suffered intervention of the institution in the private sphere of the family. Like most narrations of visits to the doctor, the author proceeds in strictly chronological order, the exact time being divided into sections. Each of these sections contains the description (or brief mention) of an examination and is concluded by definite figures, namely the exact duration of the examination and the amount to be paid for the examination in question. The costs of the individual examinations (which are not reimbursed by the health insurance funds and are therefore perceived by the immigrants as outrageously high) are given to provide precise information for interested immigrants. On the other hand, the regular sequence of figures and types of check-up emphasizes the large number of individual examinations and the costs incurred and expresses anger about them. The temporal data in the narrations emphasize the extraordinary duration of the entire process and consequently, also the burden which is imposed on the immigrants. In this way, the reader is able to understand the numerous ironic and emotional comments inserted into the posting. Finally, the two illustrations, as well as the direct renditions of speech that are repeatedly inserted, serve to illustrate and dramatize the narrative.

The scenic reconstruction of the "medical check-up" allows the author of the French blog to deal with the feeling of humiliation caused by the multitude of medical examinations required, by staging the sequence as an absurd comedy and even choosing the difficulties with the little daughter's urine specimen as the thread running through the story. The punch line the blogger gives at the end of his story no longer takes place during the check-up, i.e. the institutionally prescribed context of the medical examination, but on arrival at home, in the family. The prescribed stage of the *parcours* is thus part of the family's history, the burdensome or even annoying experience is placed within the framework of a funny anecdote about the child.

The narration of the same stage by a Latin American blogger in the following example is much less dramatic. Her narrative seems to be almost trying to play down the high burdens that have resulted from the long examinations, and yet in her comments, which are interspersed again and again, it becomes clear how humiliating and burdensome the situation was for her:

> Los exámenes médicos
>
> Como algunos ya se pudieron dar cuenta gracias al post de "timing" el pasado lunes 2 de marzo estuvimos en Bogotá prácticandonos los éxamenes médicos. Nos fue muy bien, viajamos el domingo a las 22 h por berlinas, llegamos a Bogotá a las 7 h y a las 8 h ya estabamos en el consultorio del Dr. [Proper name]. Fue el primer consultorio al que llamamos el viernes y nos dieron la cita para las 15 h del lunes. A esa hora (las 8 h) nos tomaron fotos (quedamos chistosos por aquello del viaje y de las carreras) pero luego nos dimos consuelo

con [Proper name] :p dificilmente quedariamos peor que ella jajajaja, pagamos el valor de los exámenes y de la cita, enseguida nos tomaron muestras de sangre y orina. (Consejo: vayan tempranito desayunaditos; pero sin hacer chichi. Asi sale rápidito todo y les va bien como a nosotros).

Nos dieron unas órdenes para ir a radiología en otra dirección, nos fuimos caminando hasta allá ya que no teníamos gran cosa por hacer, llegamos al sitio despues de caminar 24 cuadritas no más, a esperar a que nos llamaran para practicarnos la dichosa radiografia. Nos dieron unas batas para cubrir la desnudez de la cintura hacia arriba. Menos mal que eso es bien rápidito porque aún con esa bata **yo me sentía empelota**.

Bueno almorzamos un corrientazo por ahi cerquita y a esperar que nos entregaran los resultados. Como se demoraron dos horas en entregarlos nos devolvimos las 24 cuadritas en taxi para llegar a tiempo y sin cara de fatigados a la cita con el doc.

LLegamos a las 14h 30m más o menos y no tuvimos que esperar mucho. Primero nos pasaron a unas cabinas para -adivinen...- otra vez empelotarnos y ponernos una batica azul**, ya le estoy cogiendo práctica a eso**.

Y pues bien, nos miden, nos pesan, nos espichan la barriga, **nos palpan la garganta como buscando pepitas de oro**, un par de preguntas y eso es todo. C'est fini. [...]

Pero bueno, lo importante es que nadie puede decir que no somos juiciosos!

(Blog 13, March 2009, my emphasis)

The medical examination

As some of you could already notice thanks to the "timing" of the post last Monday, March 2, we were in Bogotá for the medical examination. It went very well, we traveled on Sunday at 10 pm by car, we arrived in Bogota at 7 am and at 8 am we were in the office of Dr. [proper name]. It was the first doctor's office we had called on Friday and we were given an appointment for 3 pm on Monday. At that time (8 am) we were photographed (we were joking about

> the trip and the race) but then we consoled ourselves with [proper name] :p we could hardly be worse off than her ha ha ha ha, we paid the fees for the examinations and the appointment, they immediately took samples of blood and urine. (Advice: have breakfast early; but without making peepee. That way everything goes quickly and you will do as well as we did).They told us to go to radiology in a different direction, we walked there because we did not have much to do, we arrived at the site after walking no more than 24 blocks, to wait for them to call us for the stupid x-rays. They gave us some gowns to cover our naked upper bodies. Luckily that's very fast because even in that robe **I felt very exposed**.
>
> Well then we had a fixed-menu lunch nearby and we waited for the results. As they took two hours to deliver them we went back the 24 blocks by taxi so we could arrive on time and without exhausted looking faces for the appointment with the doc.
>
> We arrived at 2:30 more or less and we didn't have to wait long. First they moved us to some booths to – guess what – strip again and to put on blue hospital gowns, **already I am becoming an expert at this**.
>
> And wel then, they measure us, they weigh us, they poke our bellies, **they feel our throats like they're looking for gold nuggets**, a couple of questions and that's it. *C'est fini.* [...]
>
> But the important thing is that nobody can say that we are not reasonable!

The medical examination is put into perspective as strenuous and degrading; this is merely hinted at in the brief commentaries, but reappears in the final evaluation when the immigrants are ironically categorized as "reasonable". Even if the narrative reconstruction given here does not reveal any ridicule or ironic distancing from the events, it becomes clear between the lines that this was an unpleasant experience.

In the very numerous comments that the blogger receives (more than 20 comments, some of which are answered by the blogger), the readers express their own fear of the examination, they congratulate the blogger that she has survived this stage well, but some also make sarcastic comments on the way the medical examination is conducted as in the following commentary:

> Que emoción haber salido de eso!!!
>
> se quita uno un peso de encima ademas sirve para saber que estamos sanitos!!!
>
> (Blog 13, March 16, 2009, Comment 4)
>
> What a thrill to be out of it!
>
> furthermore, it takes a weight off your shoulders to know that you are healthy!

In the "you" that includes all immigrants and the ironic commentary, the official medical examination is categorized as an imposition that unites the community all of whom have to suffer through it.

As in the interaction between patient and therapist, the support and indirect participation of the other members of the community is also an essential prerequisite for the therapeutic effect of the narrations of the bloggers. Thus, the ironic comment cited above ends with masssive encouragement by listing the few stages still to be completed and giving the blogger hope that the long wait will soon be over:

> Ya pasaste lo peor, ahora es la espera de los pasaportes. No te lo niego, la espera es dura, pero veras que pronto tendras tus pasaportes en mano y alistando tus cosas para emprender el viaje!
>
> Estare MUY pendiente de lo que pase con tus cosas!!
>
> Un abrazo
>
> (Blog 13, March 16, 2009, Comment 4)
>
> You're through the worst, now it's just the wait for the passports. I don't deny it, the wait is hard, but soon you will have your passports in your hands and will be getting your things ready to start the journey!

> I will be VERY curious about what will happen in your case!
> A hug

In the following example, another blogger talks about a particularly stressful situation: After informing her family of her plan to emigrate, it turns out that the blogger's sister and brother-in-law have health problems and are therefore more dependent on her support than before:

> Hace unos dias le comentamos el proyecto de irnos a una parte de la familia que todavia no lo sabia y no lo tomaron muy bien.... pero no nos hicieron preguntas asi que todavia no sabemos realmente que es lo que les molesta de nuestra decision [...]...
>
> Realmente me hubiese gustado poner un poco mas de energia en esta cuestion familiar pero por desgracia o por cuestiones de destino, recibimos una noticia que nos tiene muy preocupados... mi hermana y mi cunado estan pasando por un momento dificil de salud y necesitan mas que nunca de nosotros, asi que hoy toda nuestra energia, esperanza, y rezos estan totalmente dirigidos a ellos, **por eso dejamos un poco de lado lo demas**... [...]
>
> (Blog 3, Oct. 2, 2009, my emphasis)

> A few days ago we commented on the idea of going to a part of the family that still did not know and did not take it very well .... but we did not ask questions so we still do not really know what is bothering them about our decision [...]....
>
> I really would have liked to put a little more energy into this family matter but unfortunately or because of fate, we received a note that has us very worried ... at the moment my sister and my brother-in-law are going through a difficult time health-wise and need support from us more than ever, so today all our energy, hope, and prayers are totally directed to them, **so we are putting everything else a little to the side**.... [...]

She puts the personal burden into perspective from the point of view of their immigration process by postponing it in favor of a period in which all plans for the projected *parcours* are cancelled and in which the focus is on the family. The attention which the illness of her brother-in-law demands withdraws “energy, hope and prayers” from her own immigration path and returns it to the present. It is now the end of the post which is interesting. There she apologizes to the readers and thanks them explicitly for reading her words, which, as she remarks, have been therapeutic for her:

> perdon por aburrirlos pero buehh.. si llegaron al final de mi post se los agradezco.... a mi me sirvio como terapia...
>
> (ibid.)
>
> sorry to bore you but goo.. if you reached the end of my post I want to thank you .... it has served me as therapy ...

Obviously, the writing process itself and the knowledge that readers have taken note of her problems have helped her to deal with her situation. In fact, readers react with extensive comments, giving general advice from their own perspective as immigrants. The first commentator, for example, passes on appropriate advice from another immigration blog and deals with her own situation, as she herself is in a similar dilemma. She generalizes the problem of not being understood as one which applies to all immigrants and uses her own example to show that the negative attitude of relatives can change in a positive direction in the course of the immigration process:

> Hace tiempo leí en un blog que no hay que esperar que todos nos comprenda, cada uno tiene su propia historia, sus antecedentes y su forma de ver la vida; claro que cuando la incomprensión viene de nuestra sangre la cosa como que duele.
>
> La verdad cuando lo leí poco lo comprendí, hay que vivirlo, sentirlo para comprenderlo, lo importante es estar preparado para que las cosas sucedan así.
>
> Al principio del proceso pocos nos entendían, es más nos miraban con cara de “éstos están locos,” aquí vivimos muy bien, bueno, eso es un decir...digamos que tenemos una situación económica y pro-

> fesional aceptablemente estable (lo cual para los tiempos de hoy es como sacarse la lotería)pero te cuento que con el tiempo varios de nuestros parientes nos han dado completamente la razón sobre todo porque las cosas se están poniendo demasiado rojas por estos rumbos, es más, te podría decir que varios nos envidian (sobre todo los más jóvenes) y eso de que el tiempo cura las heridas es verdad, mis padres que al principio tomaron muy mal nuestros planes ahora que el momento se acerca nos apoyan totalmente y creeme que eso es una gran bendición y ayuda impagable.
>
> (ibid.)
>
> Some time ago I read in a blog that we should not expect everyone to understand us, everyone has their own history, their own background, and their own way of looking at life, of course when incomprehension comes like this from blood relatives it hurts.
>
> The truth is that when I read this, I didn't understand it much, you have to live it, feel it, to understand it, the important thing is to be prepared for things like this to happen.
>
> At the beginning of the process few people understood us, moreover they looked at us with a face like "they're crazy," here we live very well, okay, that is to say...let's say that we have an acceptably stable economic and professional situation (which for today's times is like winning in the lottery) but I tell you that over time several of our relatives have given us the complete reason, above all because things are getting too hard for our course of action, moreover, I could tell you that several envy us (especially the younger ones) and that time heals all wounds is true, my parents, who at first took our plans very badly, now that the moment is approaching fully support us and believe me this is a great blessing and invaluable help.

This creates a picture of a community of immigrants who share the same concerns and problems and also their solutions.

Numerous comments on the posts of our bloggers show that sharing common goals, problems on the way towards them, and mutual support represent a very essential aspect of the therapeutic tactics of bloggers. It shows that the supportive activities of the individual bloggers are conceived as elements of the larger blogging community.

For example, an immigrant who is already in Canada and is herself managing an immigration blog, writes the following comment to a new blogger in reaction to his second post, in which he presents himself and his motives for emigrating to Canada:

> Bien[v]enido a la blogsfera y al camino de la inmigración. creo que tus [m]otivos de partir son los mismos que el de la mayoría de los que están aquí.
> Aquí estamos para que hagas todas las preguntas de [ortsname] que quieras!
> Saludos
>
> (Blog 2, Comment April 19, 2008)
>
> Welcome to the blogosphere and to the road to immigration. I think that your motivations for leaving are the same as those of most of those who are here. We're here for you to ask all the questions you want about [name of town]!
> Greetings

The interactive process of blogging is perceived as "healing" by both the bloggers themselves and their commentators. Since the experiences narrated are almost exclusively stages of immigration, the experiences with these experiences are shared by each individual immigrant and thus the healing effect of the linguistic processing of this experience can also be of benefit to the immigrants participating in the blog whether as readers or commentators, as is expressed directly in numerous comments:

> Hola. No se quienes son, los encontramos por la web, pero quiero decirles **que ustedes con sus historias nos han ayudado mucho**, nos **dan valor de seguir adelante**, leer sus notas es como leer tambien lo que nos esta pasando y lo que estamos sintiendo. Gracias.
>
> (Blog 8, Nov. 2, 2005, comment 3, my emphasis)

> Hello, I don't know who you are, we found you on the web, but I want to tell **you that you have helped us a lot with your stories, you have given us courage to move forward**, reading your posts is like reading what is happening to us and what we are feeling. Thank you.
>
> Hola somos[Proper name] y [Proper name], los felicitamos por el blog, nos **han dado mucho animo** para empezar el proceso de inmigracion a Quebec [...].
>
> (Blog 8, Nov. 2, 2005, comment 4, my emphasis)
>
> Hello we are [proper name] and [proper name], we want to congratulate you on your blog, **you have given us a lot of encouragement** to start the process of immigration to Québec [...].

Finally, we now come to another tactic which the immigrants use in their blogs to process and cope with difficult experiences and stressful thoughts. This tactic no longer makes use of the tense of the "narrated world," but of the possibilities of the discussed world. Experiences are not reconstructed from the distance of the narrator, but rather we find here the reconstruction of processes of reflection and cognition in language, i.e. statements whose rationality the authors assume full responsibility for by making it clear to themselves and their readers that their cause is at stake, or as Weinrich (1964, 51) puts it: "tua res agitur [doing your own thing]."

These are processes of reflection on one's own actions and situation as an immigrant and the conditions and consequences of the immigration. These processes take advantage of the enlightening, epistemic function of writing. And just as with narrations, their use and therapeutic effect is not limited to the blogger, but applies to everyone involved in the interaction.

In a detailed post entitled "Is it worth all the trouble?" the author of Blog 8 describes his reflections and doubts as to whether the whole effort is worth it. Among other things, in this post he tells of the negative reaction of his family and his wife's family to their emigration plans:

> Mi madre me dijo que nosotros éramos muy arriesgados, ella no está de acuerdo, de hecho, casi nadie en la familia está de acuerdo, la familia de [Proper name] pensó que era broma, pero creo que cada vez más se convencen de que estamos decididos. Tal vez, la respuesta a la pregunta [gemeint ist die Frage im Titel des Posts] nos la den nuestros hijos, no nosotros mismos.
>
> (Blog 8, Nov. 2, 2005, excerpt)
>
> My mother told me that we were taking a lot of risks, she doesn't agree, in fact, almost nobody in the family agrees, [proper name]'s family thought it was a joke, but I think they are increasingly convinced that we are determined. Perhaps the answer to the question [viz. "Is it worth all the trouble?"] is given to us by our children, not by ourselves.

The fact that the negative reactions of the families are a burden on the immigrants is made clear by the context of the post, which poses the question of the meaning of the immigration process. In a longer commentary, a reader now shares her own reflections on this problem:

> [proper name], es muy difícil que los parientes comprendan nuestra decisión, pero sobre todo los padres...,por supuesto que a ellos no les agrada la idea que sus polluelos se alejen y sobre todo a un lugar tan lejano y desconocido como Canadá.
>
> Mira, yo estoy haciendo lo siguiente (es un jueguito mental para no agobiarme tanto con eso de que: y se me estoy equivocando? y si allá no es tan promisorio como lo pinta? y si lo mejor sería quedarme donde estoy con mi cultura, con mi familia, con mis amigos, con mi paisaje?): voy a Canadá, aprendo el idioma o los idiomas, mis hijos también aprenden el idioma, conocemos otro país, trabajamos (ya sabemos que allá no nos vamos a morir de hambre), probablemente podamos inclusive ahorrar un poco (cosa que en mi país es imposible) y si luego de de todo no nos gusta, nos regresamos a nido familiar en país de origen dentro de 4 o 5 años, pero eso sí con la ciudadanía bajo el brazo (para que nuestros hijos dejen de ser ciudadanos de quinta ante el mundo, además que les abrimos

las puertas para cuando ellos quieran emigrar como nosotros ya no les cueste lo que nos está costando a nosotros ahora). Así que no te agobies tanto con eso de que si vale la pena o nó. Somos gente joven, tómalo como si te estuvieras yendo a estudiar al extranjero: vas a estudiar idiomas, culturas, formas de trabajo, probablemente vas a estudiar algo de tu profesión también. Y si al final no funciona te regresas.

Sería interesante que les dijeras eso a tu familia también, así los tranquilizas y probablemente te comprendan un poco más.

Ánimo¡¡¡

(Blog 8, Nov. 2, 2005, commentary)

[Proper name], it's very difficult for our relatives to understand our decision, but especially our parents... of course they don't like the idea of their chicks moving away and especially to a place as far away and unknown as Canada.

Look, I'm doing the following (it's a little mental game so I don't get so overwhelmed by everything: and if I'm wrong? and if it isn't as promising there as it looks? and if the best thing would be to stay where I am in my culture, with my family, with my friends, with my landscape?): I go to Canada, I learn the language or languages, my children also learn the language, we know another country, we work (we already know that we are not going to die of hunger there), we can probably even save a little money (something that in my country is impossible) and if after all we do not like it, we return to a family nest in our country of origin in 4 or 5 years, but with citizenship under our arms (so that our children stop being citizens of the countryside rather than the world, in addition that we open the doors for them when they want to emigrate as it will not cost them as much as it costs us now). So don't get so overwhelmed with whether it's worth it or not. We're young people, take it as if you were going to study abroad: you're going to study languages, cultures, ways of working, you're probably going to study your profession some too. And if it doesn't work, you go back.

> It would be interesting if you told your family that too, that way you reassure them and they will probably understand you a little more.
>
> Cheer up!

The commentator provides the blogger with a whole set of arguments which not only serve to dispel his [the blogger's] own doubts about the immigration project, but which he can also use to reassure his family. These considerations, which the commentator herself calls "mental games," obviously apply in an identical way to her own situation. The fact that they can be transferred directly to the blogger's case proves once again that all the immigrants in the community have similar experiences and problems and that they can come to similar solutions through reflections and can thus cooperate in solving their problems.

The author of Blog 8 expresses thanks for this advice with the following words:

> [Proper name], muchísimas gracias por tus comentarios, realmente me parece muy bien poder tomar las cosas de esa manera, ya que no lo había visto de esa forma, voy a buscar poner este consejo en práctica. Saludos.
>
> (Blog 8, Nov. 2, 2005, Comment 2)

> [Proper name], thank you so much for your comments, I really think it's great to be able to take things that way, since I hadn't seen it that way, I'm going to try to put this advice into practice. Greetings.

In writing in this manner he shows that he accepts the way of thinking and reasoning proposed in the commentary to solve his own problem.

A similar problem is described in Blog 5 by a immigrant who, after three years in Canada, reflects on her life and finds that her friends, whom she left behind in Latin America, have become strangers to her. Although she has seen them several times in the meantime, an image of them has solidified in her head that has not changed in the three years since she has not been able to follow their everyday lives:

> Ayer fue nuestro troisieme anniversaire de emigrados/inmigrados.
>
> [...] Es raro, en ese momento quedo todo suspendido en el tiempo. [...] [Proper name] y [Proper name], las mismas [Proper name] y [Proper name]. [...] Pese a que volvi unas 5 veces a Argentina y los vi cada una de esas veces, en mi cerebro quedo grabada un version anterior de ellos. El mismo pelo de 2004. La misma ropa. Los mismos pensamientos. No hay cotideaneidad que vaya horadando la vision que tengo de mis amigos. Siguen siendo los mismos de hace 3 años atras. Pero no lo son.
>
> (Blog 5, May 2, 2007)
>
> Yesterday was the third anniversary as emigrants/immigrants.
>
> [...] It's strange, at that moment everything was suspended in time. [...] [proper name] and [proper name], the same [proper name] and [proper name]. [...] Even though I returned to Argentina about 5 times and saw them each time, an earlier version of them was engraved in my brain. Same hair as in 2004. The same clothes. The same thoughts. There is no everyday life that pierces the vision I have of my friends. They are still the same as 3 years ago. But they are not really.

The first of numerous comments on this post initially confirms the impression gained from personal experience and thus also the burden they bear:

> Cuanta razon tenes en eso que decis... que sentis que el mundo, tus amigos quedaron asi, como el día que los viste antes de irte con tus valijas.. aunque hayan cambiado un monton de cosas en sus vidas, para vos, el tiempo se paro!
>
> (Blog 5, April 3, 2007, Commentary)
>
> How right you are about that you say... that you feel that the world, your friends were like that, as the day you saw them before you left

> with your suitcases... although they have changed a lot of things in their lives, for you, time has stopped!

At the same time, however, she points out in consolation all the positive things that the three years in Canada have brought about:

> Felices tres años, a los dos!, por el frances que aprendieron, por la experiencia que juntaron, por la casita nueva, por los viajes.. y por todo!
>
> (Blog 5, May 3, 2007, Commentary)
>
> Happy three years, both of you!, for the French you have learned, for the experience you have gained, for the new house, for the travels... and for everything!

In this way it is possible to process and jointly cope with burdensome issues by giving descriptions and confirmations of problems along with advice and comfort to members of the blogger community who are themselves affected and receiving the same back in token.

Our concluding example shows the healing power of verbal reconstruction, which reproduces and communicates a cognitive process triggered by an emotionally charged situation. It leads us back to the prototypically stressful situation that affects all the immigrants in the Latin American blogosphere community: waiting for an official document that will open up the next stage. This example is again about waiting for the invitation to the medical, and the theme of the post is the description of blogger's own emotional concerns. The immigrant describes her growing despair in the face of the fact that she is completely helpless and subject to an arbitrary period of waiting. Her realization that many, many other immigrants are living, have lived, or will live through the same thing under similar conditions does not at first help her to bear the situation better due to some kind of feeling of a shared common destiny. On the contrary, this knowledge actually reinforces her anxiety about having to wait even longer:

> Esta semana se cumplen 7 meses que obtuve mi CSQ y entregué mis documentos al gobierno federal de Canadá, aún no tengo respuesta de las órdenes médicas, lo cual sería el próximo paso a seguir.
>
> Es una desesperación que pareciera interminable, **sé por experiencia de otras personas que es una incertidumbre muy grande** estar a la espera de estas órdenes, porque cada día aumenta más mis ganas de irme y de concretar el ideal de comenzar una nueva vida en Québec; especialmente, cuando en mi país las cosas lucen cada vez mas ajenas y lejanas a mi anhelo.
>
> No sé cuanto durará esta espera, **porque me enteré de una persona que esperó por un año y honestamente no me gustaría pasar por lo mismo**; si ese es mi destino lo aceptaré pero siento que no lo es.
>
> (Blog 12, April 17, 2007, my emphasis)
>
> This week is the seventh complete month since I obtained my CSQ and sent my documents to the federal government of Canada, I still have no response with an invitation to the medical, which would be the next step to take.
>
> The desperation seems endless, **I know from the experience of other people what great uncertainty there is** to have to wait for this invitation, because every day increases my desire to leave and to realize the ideal of starting a new life in Québec, especially when everything in my country looks increasingly alien and distant from my longing.
>
> I don't know how long this wait will last**, because I heard about a person who waited for one year and honestly I wouldn't want to go through the same thing**; if that's my destiny I'll accept it but I feel that it's not.

The consequence of these considerations about the time of waiting is a feeling of personal hopelessness and despair:

> Seguiré en esta espera que me comienza a desesperar
>
> (ibid.)

> I will continue waiting like this even though it is beginning to drive me into despair.

In the following blog entry, which she posted two weeks later and which again contains a reflection on her attitude towards the forced period of waiting, she begins to assign a new meaning to this time. Under the title “Aprovechar el Tiempo” (“Seize the day”), she first repeats almost literally her reflections from her very first post (cf. the detailed discussion of the post of April 7, 2007 in Chapter 3) and describes her reinterpretation of the waiting time as a time of preparation for her future life:

> Después de reflexionar un poco sobre esta larga espera por las ordenes médicas, llegué a la conclusión que todo tiene su razón de ser y lo mejor que puedo hacer es aprovechar este tiempo de mejorar mi francés, ahorrar y de prepararme mejor para la nueva vida que deseo tener en Montreal.
>
> (Blog 12, April 24, 2007)
>
> After reflecting a little on this long wait for the invitation to the medical, I came to the conclusion that everything has its raison d’être and the best thing I can do is to take advantage of this time to improve my French, save some money, and prepare myself better for the new life I wish to have in Montreal.

In this post, however, her considerations go even further. She refers to an article she has read about waiting times in life in general (she mentions its title, but does not give a link to the page). It is an article from an esoteric guidebook page which, with reference to the meaning of nine months pregnancy as a useful preparation time for expectant parents, gives general advice about how to use periods of waiting before important events in life as a meaningful time of preparation:

> It could be argued that life is more about the time spent waiting for something to happen than it is about something happening. What this means is that the big events in our lives are preceded by many

> days and nights of dreaming, planning, organizing, and waiting. The times of waiting in between the big events actually constitute the majority of our lives. These in-between times are anything but uneventful. In fact, they are rich with possibility and filled with opportunities for reflection and preparation. Like a pregnant woman awaiting the birth of her child, we have a finite period of time in which to prepare internally and externally for the upcoming event that will define a new chapter in our lives. [...]
>
> Nature provides the expectant parents with this time so that they can prepare the nest. This preparation plays out on many levels. Materially, a space must be created in the home and resources must be set aside for the baby's future; psychologically, a shift must occur in which the psyches of both parents agree to be responsible for a new life in the world; and emotionally, the heart must open wider to embrace and fulfill a new love.
>
> (www.dailyom.com/cgi-bin/display/articledisplay.cgi?aid=7532)

The blogger now transfers the metaphor of pregnancy as a time of preparation to her own situation in the immigration process. But unlike the author of the guide, she does not connect the content of the preparation to the expectant parents who need time to "build a nest," to adjust inwardly to their new responsibilities, and, emotionally, to enter into a new love relationship, but identifies herself with the embryo and its prenatal development:

> Es como en un artículo que leí – Exploring Our Readiness, In-Between Times – que todo tiene su tiempo y un ejemplo que daban era los meses de gestación, es necesario que un ser humano dure 9 meses en el vientre de su madre para que se le desarrollen todos sus sistemas físicos y esté preparado para la vida fuera del vientre.
>
> (Blog 12, April 24, 2007)
>
> It is like in an article I read – Exploring Our Readiness, In-Between Times – that everything has its time and an example given was the months of pregnancy, it is necessary for a human being to stay in

> the womb of his mother 9 months in order to develop all his physical systems and be prepared for life outside the womb.

Then she transfers the image of prenatal development to the growth of a plant from the invisible seed in the ground, to its gradual growth, to its transplantation to more suitable soil to grow there as a tree. The verbal reflections are supplemented by a pictorial representation of the growth of a plant:

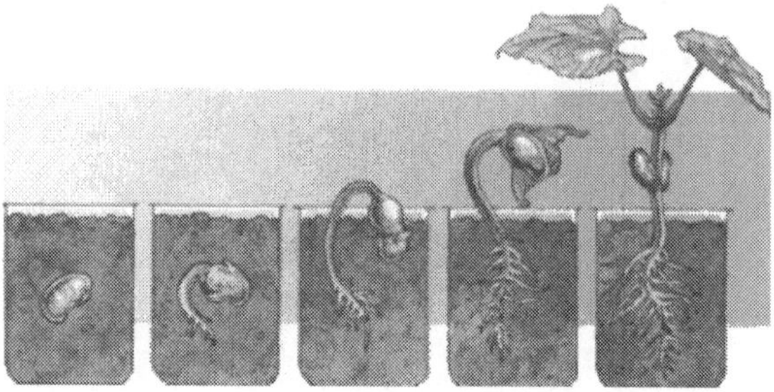

> En estos momentos creo que estoy como en la etapa de germinación, donde la semilla apenas está abriéndose para sacar sus raíces y tallo, luego irá creciendo poco a poco y posteriormente llegará el momento de ser transplantada la pequeña planta a el lugar donde crecerá como un árbol.
>
> (ibid.)
>
> Right now I think I'm in the germination stage, where the seed is just opening up to send out its roots and stem, then it will grow little by little until it is time to transplant this small plant to the place where it will grow like a tree.

The present tense of Weinrich's "discussed world" appears here as a suitable format for such promising reflections on the perception and conception of temporality, which have considerable consequences for a person's own life. We recognize here again the tactic of the everyday actor which allows him to productively reappropriate the inescapable waiting time as a meaningful creative act.

In doing so, she succeeds in reinterpreting the feeling of being subject to an unpredictable waiting period with a duration which is not rationally controllable. She manages to reshape her despair so rationally that not only the escape from her negative emotion succeeds, but positive power can even be generated. By means of reflection, a time of senseless waiting becomes a time of maturing, of becoming stronger and stronger, an evolution that makes new life possible.

At the end of the post, the blogger once again cites a pre-formed phrase about temporality, but this time it is presented as her own insight:

> Por lo tanto tengo la certeza que este tiempo de espera tiene su razón de ser.
>
> (ibid.)
>
> I am therefore certain that this waiting time has its raison d'être.

In this way, the process described here for the reader of attributing meaning becomes a general conceptualization of time within the framework of the immigration process and thus an identity-forming element of the community of blogging immigrants as a whole: In the image of the plant that grows from the inconspicuous seed and is finally transplanted into an environment in which it can grow into a strong tree, this blogger has created an image of the period of immigration that has completely detached itself from the image of the *parcours d'immigration* in the discourse of official immigration policy and replaced it with the notion of natural development and free growth.

The author of Blog 10 expresses himself even more clearly when he compares the entire immigration process with psychotherapy that enables a complete redefinition of one's own identity:

> ***La migración es una de las pocas circunstancias en la vida que permite reinventarse completamente como individuo***, algo así como una psicoterapia que al final es exitosa (nadie dijo fácil, dije

> exitosa). Piense que poca gente en este mundo tiene la posibilidad de reinventar su vida, y piense que poca gente tiene la posibilidad de emigrar a un país como Canadá.
>
> (Blog 10, Feb. 4, 2005; my emphasis)
>
> **Immigration is one of the few circumstances in life that allows someone to completely reinvent themselves as an individual**, something like psychotherapy that is ultimately successful (no one said easy, I said successful). Remember that few people in this world have the possibility to reinvent their lives, and remember that few people have the possibility of emigrating to a country like Canada.

It is undoubtedly more than just a coincidence that this man, the most famous Latin American immigration blogger, ends this thought with the image of immigration as the re-writing of his life as a novel:

> Ahora tiene la posibilidad de re-escribir toda la novela de vuelta.
>
> (ibid.)
>
> Now you have the chance to rewrite the whole novel from the beginning.

6. Conclusion

> era una decision de cambio total de vida, de pais, de estado civil, de idioma, de trabajo....de TODO.......Radicalmente.
>
> (Blog 1, January 2009, no date)
>
> It was a decision of total change of life, of country, of marital status, of language, of work....of EVERYTHING........Radical.
>
> Tengo la sensación de que nada es lo mismo después de la decisión de emigrar. Realmente uno, si está de veras vivo, cambia. Y emigrar es un baldazo de cambios.
>
> (Blog 7, 1.11.2006, commentary)
>
> I have the feeling that nothing is the same since the decision to emigrate. There's really one thing, if you're truly alive, you change. And emigrating is a bucket full of change.

The decision to emigrate to another country changes almost everything in a person's life. Therefore, if we have looked in the previous chapters at time, its perception, its reflection, and its verbal shaping by immigrants, we have, as it were, arbitrarily selected a single aspect from the totality of change in order to illustrate in exemplary fashion what structures this change generates in the way the people involved communicate, what constructions and reconstructions of temporality within the emigration process are expressed linguistically and therefore become observable. Consequently, time represents only one single sample from the totality of the changes which have transpired.

In the past chapters, this sample has shown that in the narrative procedures and interactional linguistic processes of blog communications there are structures which can be identified which are related to the special biographical situation of immigrants. Immigration to Québec is subject to fixed rules and regulations that the immigration authorities impose on all immigrants. At the center of these rules is the *parcours*, which consists of numerous individual stages, each of which in turn takes place according to fixed conditions, including a predetermined time structure. In the communication of the blogging immigrants, this *parcours* is reconstructed as a phase in which the normal course of everyday life is suspended in favor of a time of waiting and insecurity. Here a series of intermediate goals can be identified whose final goal, actual immigration, often proves to be only a further intermediate step for the actors involved on a longer-term path of integration in the host society.

In this context, the narrative itself and the reflection of stressful experiences are reconstructed and interactively processed by the actor community in blogs. This can be recognized as a joint coping strategy that not only helps the individual to process the experiences, but at the same time permits a collectively valid appropriation and reinterpretation of the immigration process, which contribute essentially to the cooperative construction of a new identity.

7. Annex: Overview of the Blogs Used[8]

Blog 1: Colnada-Canombia
(http://colnadacanombia.blogspot.com)
Blog 2: Verdades a medias
(http://leo-jajajajaja.blogspot.com)
Blog 3: Los loquitos en Canadá
(http://loquitosrumboacanada.blogspot.com)
Blog 4: Los Marge en Canadá: argentinos en Canadá
(http://losmarge.com.ar)
Blog 5: Mi vida en otro lado
(http://mividaenotrolado.blogspot.com)
Blog 6: Pereiranos al Canadá
(http://pereiranosalcanada.blogspot.com)
Blog 7: Una voz en la ciudad de Québec
(http://unavozenquebec.blogspot.com)
Blog 8: Vamos para Quebec
(http://vamospaquebec.blogspot.com)
Blog 9: Volar a Quebec
(http://volaraquebec.blogspot.com)
Blog 10: Los Ziegler En Canadá
(http://loszieglerencanada.com)
Blog 11: Vivo en Canadá
(https://www.vivoencanada.com/)
Blog 12: araguaney-maple
(http://araguaney-maple.blogspot.com)
Blog 13: Contandodiaz
(http://contandodiaz.blogspot.com/)
Blog 14: Mexicanoacanada
(http://mexicanoacanada.blogspot.com)
French Blog: http://cymico.over-blog.com

8 The corpus was collected in the years 2006-2013. The last accesses took place in September 2013. Some of the blogs are no longer available online.

8. Works Cited

Antaki, Charles and Susan Widdicombe, ed. 1998. *Identities in Talk*. London: Sage.

Baynham, Mike and Anna De Fina. 2017. "Narrative analysis in migrant and transnational contexts." In *Researching Multilingualism. Critical and Ethnographic Perspectives*, ed. Marilyn Martin-Jones and Deirdre Martin, 31–45. Abingdon and New York: Routledge.

Berger, Peter L. and Thomas Luckmann. 1966a. *The Social Construction of Reality: A Treatise in the Sociology of Knowledge*. Garden City, NY: Doubleday.

Berger, Peter L. and Thomas Luckmann. 1966b. *Die gesellschaftliche Konstruktion der Wirklichkeit*. Frankfurt a.M.: Fischer.

Bhabha, Homi K. 2000. *Die Verortung der Kultur*. Tübingen: Stauffenburg.

Bhabha, Homi K. 1994. *The Location of Culture*. New York: Routledge

Brockmeier, Jens. 2015. "Erfahrung und Erzählung." In *Narrative Bewältigung von Trauma und Verlust*, ed. Carl Eduard Scheidt, Gabriele Lucius-Hoene, Anja Stukenbrock, and Elisabeth Waller, 1–13. Stuttgart: Schattauer.

Bühler, Karl. 1934. *Sprachtheorie. Die Darstellungsfunktion der Sprache*. Jena: G. Fischer.

Catani, Stephani and Frank Neuner. 2020. "Kein Weg ins Jetzt. Die Posttraumatische Belastungsstörung und die Literatur der Gegenwart." In *Angstsprachen. Interdisziplinäre Zugänge zur kommunikativen Auseinandersetzung mit Angst*, ed. Barbara Frank-Job and Michael Joachim, 13–33. Wiesbaden: Springer VS.

Charon, Rita. 2008. *Narrative Medicine. Honoring the Stories of Illness*. Oxford: Oxford University Press.

de Certeau, Michel. 1988. *The Practice of Everyday Life*. Berkeley/Los Angeles: University of Califormia Press.

de Certeau, Michel. 1990. *L'Invention du Quotidien*. Vol. 1. Paris: Arts de Faire.

De Fina, Anna. 2011. "Discourse and identity." In *Discourse Studies. A Multidisciplinary Introduction*. 2nd edition, ed. Teun A. van Dijk, 263–282. London: Sage.

De Fina, Anna, Deborah Schiffrin, and Michael Bamberg, ed. 2006a. *Discourse and Identity*. Cambridge: Cambridge University Press.

De Fina, Anna, Deborah Schiffrin, and Michael Bamberg. 2006b. "Editor's Introduction (Part IV)." In *Discourse and Identity*, ed. Anna De Fina, Deborah Schiffrin, and Michael Bamberg, 345-350. Cambridge: Cambridge University Press

Enderli, Samuel. 2014. *Weblogs als Medium elektronischer Schriftlichkeit. Eine systemtheoretische Analyse*. Hamburg: Diplomica Verlag.

Frank-Job, Barbara and Bettina Kluge. 2015. "Multilingual Practices in Identity Construction: Virtual Communities of Immigrants to Quebec." In *Transcultural Mobility*. fiar – Forum for Inter-American Research 8.1: 85–108.

Frank-Job, Barbara and Bettina Kluge. 2012. "Die kooperative Konstruktion von Identitäten im virtuellen Kommunkationsraum des Web 2.0: Blogs zum Thema Migration nach Québec." In *Sprache und Öffentlichkeit in realen und virtuellen Räumen*, ed. Annette Gerstenberg, Claudia Polzin-Haumann, and Dietmar Osthus, 47–78. Bonn: Romanistischer Verlag.

Frank-Job, Barbara, Alexander Mehler, and Tilmann Sutter, ed. 2013. *Die Dynamik sozialer und sprachlicher Netzwerke. Konzepte, Methoden und empirische Untersuchungen an Beispielen des WWW*. Wiesbaden: Springer VS.

Freeman, Mark. 2015. "'Nachträglichkeit', traumatisch und nicht-traumatisch: Erinnerung, Erzählung und das Mysterium der Ursprünge." In *Narrative Bewältigung von Trauma und Verlust*, ed. Carl Eduard Scheidt, Gabriele Lucius-Hoene, Anja Stukenbrock, and Elisabeth Waller, 14–25. Stuttgart: Schattauer.

Garfinkel, Harold. 2002. *Working Out Durkheim's Aphorism: Ethnomethodology's Program*. Lanham, MD: Rowman and Littlefield.

Hahn, Alois. 1982. "Zur Soziologie der Beichte und anderer Formen institutionalisierter Bekenntnisse: Selbstthematisierung und Zivilisationsprozess." *Kölner Zeitschrift für Soziologie und Sozialpsychologie* 34: 407–434.

Hahn, Alois. 1987. "Identität und Selbstthematisierung." In *Selbstthematisierung und Selbstzeugnis: Bekenntnis und Geständnis*, ed. Alois Hahn and Volker Kapp, 9–24. Frankfurt a.M.: Suhrkamp.

Hall, Stuart. 1996. "The question of cultural identity." In *Modernity and its Futures*, ed. Stuart Hall, David Held, and Anthony McGrew, 274–316. Cambridge: Polity Press in association with the Open University.

Housley, William and Richard Fitzgerald. 2009. "Membership categorization, culture and norms in action." *Discourse & Society* 20.3: 345–362.

Kallmeyer, Werner. 1981. "Gestaltungsorientiertheit in Alltagserzählungen." In *Erzählung und Erzählforschung im 20. Jahrhundert*, ed. Rolf Kloepfer and Gisela Janetzke-Dillner, 409–429. Stuttgart: Schattauer.

Kluge, Bettina. 2011. "'Mi vida en otro lado'. Identitätskonstitution in den Blogs lateinamerikanischer Immigranten in Québec." In *Hybridität, Transkulturalität und Kreolisierung: Innovation und Wandel in Kultur, Sprache und Literatur Lateinamerikas* (Jahrbuch des Österreichischen Lateinamerika-Instituts, Vol. 14), ed. E. Gugenberger and K. Sartingen, 193–219. Vienna, Münster: LIT-Verlag.

Kluge, Bettina. 2012. *Referential ambiguity in interaction. Establishing generic reference with second person pronouns in the Romance languages*, unpublished post-doctoral dissertation, Universität Bielefeld.

Kluge, Bettina. 2013. "'La integración es una negociación permanente'. Die Quebecer Integrationsdebatte in der Blogosphäre der lateinamerikanischen Immigranten in Québec." In *America Romana: Perspektiven transarealer Vernetzungen* (America Romana, Vol. 4), ed. Christine Felbeck, Johannes Kramer, and Andre Klump, 39–58. Frankfurt a.M.: Peter Lang.

Kluge, Bettina. 2015. "The joint construction of a supra-national Latin American identity in the Latin American blogging community in Quebec." In *A Sociolinguistics of Diaspora: Latino Practices, Identities and Ideologies*, ed. Rosina Márquez Reiter and Luisa Martín Rojo, 181–195. London: Routledge.

Labov, William and Joshua Waletzky. 1973. "Erzählanalyse: mündliche Versionen persönlicher Erfahrung." In *Literaturwissenschaft und Linguistik*, Vol. 2, ed. Jens Ihwe, 78–126. Frankfurt a.M.: Fischer-Athenäum Taschenbuch.

Lucius-Hoene, Gabriele. 2000. "Konstruktionen und Rekonstruktionen narrativer Identität." *Forum Qualitative Sozialforschung* 1.2. http://nbn-resolving.de/urn:nbn:de:0114-fqs0002189.

Lucius-Hoene, Gabriele and Arnulf Deppermann. 2002. *Rekonstruktion narrativer Identität. Ein Arbeitsbuch zur Analyse narrativer Interviews.* Opladen: Leske + Budrich.

Lucius-Hoene, Gabriele and Arnulf Deppermann. 2004a. "Narrative Identität und Positionierung." *Gesprächsforschung – Online-Zeitschrift zur verbalen Interaktion* 5: 166-183. http://www.gespraechsforschung-ozs.de/heft2004/ga-lucius.pdf.

Lucius-Hoene, Gabriele and Arnulf Deppermann. 2004b. *Rekonstruktion narrativer Identität. Ein Arbeitsbuch zur Analyse narrativer Interviews*. 2nd edition. Wiesbaden: Springer VS.

Lucius-Hoene, Gabriele and Arnulf Deppermann. 2008. "Positionierung als Verfahren der Interaktionskontrolle. Thematisierung, De-Thematisierung und symbolische Aufhebung des Abschieds in der letzten Stunde der Therapie 'Amalie'". *Psychotherapie und Sozialwissenschaft* 10: 21-30.

McAdams, Dan P. 2006. *The Redemptive Self: Stories Americans Live by*. New York: Oxford University Press.

Mishler, Elliot G. 2009. "Narrative and identity: the double arrow of time." In *Discourse and Identity*, ed. Anna De Fina, Deborah Schiffrin, and Michael Bamberg, 30–47. Cambridge: CUP.

Neuner, Frank, Maggie Schauer, and Thomas Elbert. 2009. "Narrative Exposition und andere narrative Verfahren." In *Posttraumatische Belastungsstörungen.* 3rd edition, ed. Andreas Maercker, 302–318. Heidelberg: Springer.

Opp, Joachim and Barbara Frank-Job. 2017. "Hypothesen zur Genese dissoziativer Anfälle anhand der Anfallsschilderungen." *Zeitschrift für Epileptologie* 30.1: 34–38.

Opp, Joachim, Barbara Frank-Job, and Heike Knerich. 2015. "Linguistische Analyse von Anfallsschilderungen zur Unterscheidung epileptischer und dissoziativer Anfälle." *Neuropädiatrie in Klinik und Praxis* 14.1: 2–10.

Quasthoff, Uta. 2001. "Erzählen als interaktive Gesprächsstruktur." In *Text- und Gesprächslinguistik. Ein internationales Handbuch zeitgenössischer Forschung*. Vol. 2, ed. Klaus Brinker, Gerd Antos, Wolfgang Heinemann, and Sven F. Sager, 1293–1309. Berlin and New York: de Gruyter.

Quasthoff, Uta. 1981. "Zuhöreraktivitäten beim konversationellen Erzählen." In *Dialogforschung*, ed. P. Schröder and H. Steger, 287–313. Düsseldorf: Jahrbuch 1980 des Instituts für deutsche Sprache.

Quasthoff, Uta. 1980. *Erzählen in Gesprächen. Linguistische Untersuchungen zu Strukturen und Funktionen am Beispiel einer Kommunikationsform des Alltags*, Tübingen: Narr.

Raible, Wolfgang. 2004. "Über das Entstehen der Gedanken beim Schreiben." In *Performativität und Medialität*, ed. Sybille Krämer, 191–214. München: Fink.

Raible, Wolfgang. 1999. *Kognitive Aspekte des Schreibens* (Schriften der Philosophisch-historischen Klasse der Heidelberger Akademie der Wissenschaften, Vol. 14). Heidelberg: Winter.

Ricoeur, Paul. 1980. "Narrative Time." *Critical Inquiry* 7.1: 169–190.

Sack, Martin. 2015. "Narrative Arbeit im Kontext 'schonender Traumatherapie.'" In *Narrative Bewältigung von Trauma und Verlust*, ed. Carl Eduard Scheidt, Gabriele Lucius-Hoene, Anja Stukenbrock, and Elisabeth Waller, 150–160. Stuttgart: Schattauer.

Schauer, Maggie, Frank Neuner, and Thomas Elbert. 2011. *Narrative Exposure Therapy. A Short-term Treatment for Traumatic Stress Disorders.* 2nd revised and expanded edition. Cambridge and Göttingen: Hogrefe & Huber Publishers.

Schauer, Maggie, Frank Neuner, and Thomas Elbert. 2005. *Narrative Exposure Therapy: A Short-Term Intervention for Traumatic Stress Disorders after War, Terror or Torture.* Göttingen: Hogrefe & Huber Publishers.

Schegloff, Emanuel A. 2007. "A tutorial on membership categorization." In *Journal of Pragmatics* 39.3: 462-482.

Scheidt, Carl Eduard and Gabriele Lucius-Hoene. 2015. "Kategorisierung und narrative Bewältigung bindungsbezogener Traumaerfahrungen im Erwachsenenbindungsinterview." In *Narrative Bewältigung von Trauma und Verlust*, ed. Carl Eduard Scheidt, Gabriele Lucius-Hoene, Anja Stukenbrock, and Elisabeth Waller, 26–38. Stuttgart: Schattauer.

Scheidt, Carl Eduard, Gabriele Lucius-Hoene, Anja Stukenbrock, and Elisabeth Waller, ed. 2015. *Narrative Bewältigung von Trauma und Verlust*. Stuttgart: Schattauer.

Schmidt, Jan. 2005. *Praktiken des Bloggens, Berichte der Forschungsstelle* "Neue Kommunikationsmedien," Nr. 05–01. http://www.fonk-bamberg.de/pdf/fonkbericht0501.pdf.

Schütz, Alfred. 1971. *Collected Papers I* (Phaenomenologica, Vol. 11). Den Haag: Martinus Nijhoff.

Schütz, Alfred and Thomas Luckmann. 1979. *Strukturen der Lebenswelt.* Vol. 1. Frankfurt a.M.: Suhrkamp.

Weinrich, Harald. 1964. *Tempus. Besprochene und erzählte Welt.* Stuttgart: Kohlhammer.

Wenger, Etienne. 1998. *Communities of Practice: Learning, Meaning, and Identity*. Cambridge: Cambridge University Press.

Willems, Herbert. 1999. "Institutionelle Selbstthematisierungen und Identitätsbildungen im Modernisierungsprozess." In *Identität und Moderne*, ed. Herbert Willems and Alois Hahn, 62–101. Frankfurt a.M.: Suhrkamp.

Inter-American Studies
Cultures – Societies – History

Estudios Interamericanos
Culturas – Sociedades – Historia

This interdisciplinary series examines national and transnational issues in the cultures, societies, and histories of the Americas. It creates a forum for a critical academic dialogue between North and South, promoting an inter-American paradigm that shifts the scholarly focus from methodological nationalism to the wider context of the Western Hemisphere.

Vol. 1
Raab, Josef, Sebastian Thies, and Daniela Noll-Opitz, eds. *Screening the Americas: Narration of Nation in Documentary Film / Proyectando las Américas: Narración de la nación en el cine documental.* 2011. 472 pp.

WVT Wissenschaftlicher Verlag Trier	ISBN 978-3-86821-331-7	€ 29,50
Bilingual Press / Editorial Bilingüe	ISBN 978-1-931010-83-2	$ 29.50

Vol. 2
Raussert, Wilfried, and Michelle Habell-Pallán, eds. *Cornbread and Cuchifritos: Ethnic Identity Politics, Transnationalization, and Transculturation in American Urban Popular Music.* 2011. 292 pp.

WVT Wissenschaftlicher Verlag Trier	ISBN 978-3-86821-265-5	€ 29,50
Bilingual Press / Editorial Bilingüe	ISBN 978- 1-931010-80-1	$ 29.50

Vol. 3
Butler, Martin, Jens Martin Gurr, and Olaf Kaltmeier, eds. *EthniCities: Metropolitan Cultures and Ethnic Identities in the Americas.* 2011. 268 pp.

WVT Wissenschaftlicher Verlag Trier	ISBN 978-3-86821-310-2	€ 29,50
Bilingual Press / Editorial Bilingüe	ISBN 978-1-931010-81-8	$ 29.50

Vol. 4
Gurr, Jens Martin, and Wilfried Raussert, eds. *Cityscapes in the Americas and Beyond: Representations of Urban Complexity in Literature and Film.* 2011. 300 pp.

WVT Wissenschaftlicher Verlag Trier	ISBN 978-3-86821-324-9	€ 29,50
Bilingual Press / Editorial Bilingüe	ISBN 978-1-931010-82-5	$ 29.50

Vol. 5

Kirschner, Luz Angélica, ed. *Expanding* Latinidad*: An Inter-American Perspective*. 2012. 292 pp.

WVT Wissenschaftlicher Verlag Trier	ISBN 978-3-86821-309-6	€ 29,50
Bilingual Press / Editorial Bilingüe	ISBN 978-1-931010-84-9	$ 29.50

Vol. 6

Raussert, Wilfried, and Graciela Martínez-Zalce, eds. *(Re)Discovering 'America': Road Movies and Other Travel Narratives in North America / (Re)Descubriendo 'América': Road movie y otras narrativas de viaje en América del Norte*. 2012. 252 pp.

WVT Wissenschaftlicher Verlag Trier	ISBN 978-3-86821-384-3	€ 29,50
Bilingual Press / Editorial Bilingüe	ISBN 978-1-931010-91-7	$ 29.50

Vol. 7

Kaltmeier, Olaf, ed. *Transnational Americas: Envisioning Inter-American Area Studies in Globalization Processes*. 2013. 278 pp.

WVT Wissenschaftlicher Verlag Trier	ISBN 978-3-86821-415-4	€ 29,50
Bilingual Press / Editorial Bilingüe	ISBN 978-1-931010-92-4	$ 29.50

Vol. 8

Raab, Josef, and Alexander Greiffenstern, eds. *Interculturalism in North America: Canada, the United States, Mexico, and Beyond.* 2013. 312 pp.

WVT Wissenschaftlicher Verlag Trier	ISBN 978-3-86821-460-4	€ 29,50
Bilingual Press / Editorial Bilingüe	ISBN 978-1-931010-99-3	$ 29.50

Vol. 9

Raab, Josef, ed. *New World Colors: Ethnicity, Belonging, and Difference in the Americas*. 2014. 418 pp.

WVT Wissenschaftlicher Verlag Trier	ISBN 978-3-86821-461-1	€ 29,50
Bilingual Press / Editorial Bilingüe	ISBN 978-1-939743-00-8	$ 39.50

Vol. 10

Roth, Julia. *Occidental Readings, Decolonial Practices: A Selection on Gender, Genre, and Coloniality in the Americas*. 2014. 284 pp.

WVT Wissenschaftlicher Verlag Trier	ISBN 978-3-86821-446-8	€ 26,50
Bilingual Press / Editorial Bilingüe	ISBN 978-1-939743-07-7	$ 32.50

Vol. 11

Thies, Sebastian, Gabriele Pisarz-Ramirez, and Luzelena Gutiérrez de Velasco, eds. *Of Fatherlands and Motherlands: Gender and Nation in the Americas / De Patrias y Matrias: Género y nación en las Américas*. 2015. 344 pp.

WVT Wissenschaftlicher Verlag Trier	ISBN 978-3-86821-528-1	€ 29,50
Bilingual Press / Editorial Bilingüe	ISBN 978-1-939743-08-4	$ 39.50

Vol. 12

Fuchs, Rebecca. *Caribbeanness as a Global Phenomenon: Junot Díaz, Edwidge Danticat, and Cristina García*. 2014. 298 pp.

WVT Wissenschaftlicher Verlag Trier	ISBN 978-3-86821-533-5	€ 26,50
Bilingual Press / Editorial Bilingüe	ISBN 978-1-939743-09-1	$ 32.50

Vol. 13

Andres, Julia. *¡Cuéntame algo! – Chicana Narrative Beyond the Borderlands*. 2015. 202 pp.

WVT Wissenschaftlicher Verlag Trier	ISBN 978-3-86821-569-4	€ 25,00
Bilingual Press / Editorial Bilingüe	ISBN 978-1-939743-11-4	$ 28.50

Vol. 14

Hertlein, Saskia. *Tales of Transformation: Emerging Adulthood, Migration, and Ethnicity in Contemporary American Literature*. 2014. 228 pp.

WVT Wissenschaftlicher Verlag Trier	ISBN 978-3-86821-570-0	€ 25,00
Bilingual Press / Editorial Bilingüe	ISBN 978-1-939743-10-7	$ 31.50

Vol. 15

Raab, Josef, and Saskia Hertlein, eds. *Spaces – Communities – Discourses: Charting Identity and Belonging in the Americas*. 2016. 382 pp.

WVT Wissenschaftlicher Verlag Trier	ISBN 978-3-86821-590-8	€ 29,50
Bilingual Press / Editorial Bilingüe	ISBN 978-1-939743-13-8	$ 39.50

Vol. 16

Mehring, Frank, ed. *The Mexico Diary: Winold Reiss between Vogue Mexico and Harlem Renaissance. An Illustrated Trilingual Edition with Commentary and Musical Interpretation* (includes color plates and audio CD). 2016. 244 pp.

WVT Wissenschaftlicher Verlag Trier	ISBN 978-3-86821-594-6	€ 29,50
Bilingual Press / Editorial Bilingüe	ISBN 978-1-939743-14-5	$ 39.50

Vol. 17

Raussert, Wilfried, Brian Rozema, Yolanda Campos, and Marius Littschwager, eds. *Key Tropes in Inter-American Studies: Perspectives from the* forum for inter-american research (fiar). 2015. 374 pp.

WVT Wissenschaftlicher Verlag Trier	ISBN 978-3-86821-627-1	€ 29,50
Bilingual Press / Editorial Bilingüe	ISBN 978-1-939743-16-9	$ 39.50

Vol. 19

Rehm, Lukas, Jochen Kemner, and Olaf Kaltmeier, eds. *Politics of Entanglement in the Americas: Connecting Transnational Flows and Local Perspectives*. 2017. 226 pp.

WVT Wissenschaftlicher Verlag Trier	ISBN 978-3-86821-675-2	€ 27,50
Bilingual Press / Editorial Bilingüe	ISBN 978-1-939743-17-6	$ 32.50

Vol. 20
Britt Arredondo, Christopher. *Imperial Idiocy: A Reflection on Forced Displacement in the Americas*. 2017. 194 pp.
WVT Wissenschaftlicher Verlag Trier ISBN 978-3-86821-706-3 € 26,50
Bilingual Press / Editorial Bilingüe ISBN 978-1-939743-20-6 $ 30.00

Vol. 21
Schemien, Alexia. *Of Virgins, Curanderas, and Wrestler Saints: Un/Doing Religion in Contemporary Mexican American Literature*. 2018. 218 pp.
WVT Wissenschaftlicher Verlag Trier ISBN 978-3-86821-724-7 € 27,50
Bilingual Press / Editorial Bilingüe ISBN 978-1-939743-22-0 $ 32.50

Vol. 22
Fulger, Maria Diana. *The Cuban Post-Socialist Exotic: Contemporary U.S. American Travel Narratives about Cuba.* 2020. 266 pp.
WVT Wissenschaftlicher Verlag Trier ISBN 978-3-86821-769-8 € 32,50
Bilingual Press / Editorial Bilingüe ISBN 978-1-939743-27-5 $ 36.00

Vol. 24
Kaltmeier, Olaf, Mirko Petersen, Wilfried Raussert, and Julia Roth, eds. *Cherishing the Past, Envisioning the Future. Entangled Practises of Heritage and Utopia in the Americas.* 2021. 176 pp.
WVT Wissenschaftlicher Verlag Trier ISBN 978-3-86821-804-6 € 23,50
UNO University of New Orleans Press ISBN 978-1-60801-206-0 $ 27.50

Vol. 26
Raussert, Wilfried. *'What's Going On': How Music Shapes the Social.* 2021. 224 pp.
WVT Wissenschaftlicher Verlag Trier ISBN 978-3-86821-811-4 € 28,50
UNO University of New Orleans Press ISBN 978-1-60801-199-5 $ 34.00

Vol. 27
Frank-Job, Barbara. *Immigration as a Process: Temporality Concepts in Blogs of Latin American Immigrants to Québec.* 2021. 138 pp.
WVT Wissenschaftlicher Verlag Trier ISBN 978-3-86821-820-6 € 20,00
UNO University of New Orleans Press ISBN 978-1-60801-215-2 $ 24.00

Vol. 28
Roth, Julia. *Can Feminism Trump Populism? Right-Wing Trends and Intersectional Contestations in the Americas.* 2021. 168 pp.
WVT Wissenschaftlicher Verlag Trier ISBN 978-3-86821-821-3 € 23,00
UNO University of New Orleans Press ISBN 978-1-60801-205-3 $ 26.00

Vol. 30

Buitrago Valencia, Clara. *Missionaries: Migrants or Expatriates? Guatemalan Pentecostal Leaders in Los Angeles.* 2021. 236 pp.

WVT Wissenschaftlicher Verlag Trier	ISBN 978-3-86821-818-3	€ 28,50
UNO University of New Orleans Press	ISBN 978-1-60801-210-7	$ 34.50

Vol. 31

Schwabe, Nicole. *De-Centering History Education: Creating Knowledge of Global Entanglements.* 2021. 92 pp.

WVT Wissenschaftlicher Verlag Trier	ISBN 978-3-86821-828-2	€ 18,00
UNO University of New Orleans Press	ISBN 978-1-60801-214-5	$ 21.00

Vol. 32

Manke, Albert. *Coping with Discrimination and Exclusion. Experiences of Free Chinese Migrants in the Americas in a Transregional and Diachronic Perspective.* 2021. 162 pp.

WVT Wissenschaftlicher Verlag Trier	ISBN 978-3-86821-829-9	€ 23,00
UNO University of New Orleans Press	ISBN 978-1-60801-207-7	$ 27.00

Vol. 33

Rohland, Eleonora. *Entangled Histories and the Environment? Socio-Environmental Transformations in the Caribbean, 1492-1800.* 2021. 92 pp.

WVT Wissenschaftlicher Verlag Trier	ISBN 978-3-86821-833-6	€ 18,00
UNO University of New Orleans Press	ISBN 978-1-60801-208-4	$ 21.00

Vol. 34

Kaltmeier, Olaf. *National Parks from North to South. An Entangled History of Conservation and Colonization in Argentina.* 2021. 208 pp.

WVT Wissenschaftlicher Verlag Trier	ISBN 978-3-86821-834-3	€ 27,50
UNO University of New Orleans Press	ISBN 978-1-60801-204-6	$ 32.50

Vol. 35

Raussert, Wilfried. *Off the Grid. Art Practices and Public Space.* 2021. 232 pp.

WVT Wissenschaftlicher Verlag Trier	ISBN 978-3-86821-835-0	€ 29,50
UNO University of New Orleans Press	ISBN 978-1-60801-213-8	$ 34.50

Vol. 36

Ravasio, Paola. *This Train Is Not Bound to Glory. A Study of Literary Trainscapes.* 2021. 114 pp.

WVT Wissenschaftlicher Verlag Trier	ISBN 978-3-86821-836-7	€ 18,00
UNO University of New Orleans Press	ISBN 978-1-60801-216-9	$ 21.00

Vol. 37

Schäfer, Heinrich Wilhelm. *Protestant 'Sects' and the Spirit of (Anti-)Imperialism. Religious Entanglements in the Americas.* 2021. 242 pp.

WVT Wissenschaftlicher Verlag Trier	ISBN 978-3-86821-855-8	€ 29,50
UNO University of New Orleans Press	ISBN 978-1-60801-209-1	$ 34.50